Quick & Easy
Way to Learn Hindi

Pt. Aditya Nand

Qualis Books
11/83 Punjabi Bagh
New Delhi - 110 026

ISBN No. 81-87838-01-9

1st Publish in Qualis Books 2003
Quick & Easy way to Learn Hindi

Price : Rs. 95/-

cover design by : The Exact Page
Published by
Qualis Books
11/83 Punjabi Bagh
New Delhi - 110 026
Phone : 5423010

Printed in India at
Kay Kay Printers
New Delhi

Quick & Easy Way to Learn Hindi

Hindi is India's national and most widely-spoken language. It is also India's link with the communities of Indian origin spread over all the continents and many island nations.

This book is specially designed to self-teach Hindi to those who want it. Non-Hindi speakers, specially the tourists from abroad, will find it an excellent, accurate and easy-to-handle tool for language learning. Avoiding the intricacies of grammar, it goes to the subject directly and helps the readers pick up the spoken language for everyday use.

If Hindi is the language you want to learn, this is the ideal book for you. No hassles, just an easy, straightforward method to get on with Hindi as a spoken and written language.

It is the imperative need of the time that people should come close to each other so that they may understand each other well. Language is the only bridge to bring the people in close contact. Tourist traffic in India is increasing day-by-day. This book will prove handy for them and they will learn Hindi in a couple of days. We have tried to cater everyday subjects in a very common, simple and accurtae vocabulary of English, Hindi and its pronunciation in Roman. This method will help the foreigh tourists very much.

Author of this book is a renowned journalist and linguist. He has many National and International awards to his credit. We are sure that this book will prove as a lighthouse for foreign users of the language.

To Hindi-Learners

Language is a vehicle to disseminate knowledge as well as the main communication source. Hindi is spoken by a large majority in India. A tourist who comes to this vast, multilingual and multiracial country cannot learn so many languages but, if he has got some knowledge of Hindi he can well converse with Indian masses because Hindi-knowing people are living in every nook and corner of this country from Kashmir to Kanyakumari. Therefore, it is essential to have a workable knowledge of Hindi for every foreigner to get through the everyday, ordeal of communication.

I have gone through some Hindi-teaching books and found that they have dealt with grammar formally and have given through a vocabulary. I have adopted a middle way and dealt with grammar in a separate chapter. I have given more stress on vocabulary which is helpful for conversation. This method will prove more useful for the visitors from European countries also such as France, Germany and other areas who are not well acquainted with English. I have tried to touch every aspect with which the tourist has to deal. These subjects are dealt with in very simple sentences.

One of the plus points of Hindi is that it is pronounced as it is written. No letter is silent as it is in English. I have given pronunciations in Roman so that the reader would not feel any difficulty.

CONTENTS

A Chart of Matras

PART 3

   I Social Phraseology / Administrative Terms
  II Foreign words
 III Telegraphic Greetings
 IV Short Letters
  V Popular Proverbs

PART 4

Conversations I Meeting & Parting II Pleasing & Surprising III Anger
& Blame IV Bed Tea V Breakfast VI Lunch VII Evening Tea VIII Dinner
IX Stroll X Visit XI Invitation XII Travel XIII Hotel XIV Purchase
XV Laundry

PART 5

Grammar
(1) Parts of Speech (2) Nouns-Pronouns-Verbs-Adjectives-Adverbs-
Conjunctions-Prepositions-Interjections (3) Voice (4) Numbers
(5) Genders (6) Clauses (7) Use of should, ought, must, lest, so that
(8) Use of conservative verbs (9) Use of gerund, participle & Infinitive
(10) Use of Article (11) Use of important Prepositions (12) Use of
some conjunctions (13) Use of am to, is to, are to, was to, were to,
has to, have to, had to, use to, used to, about to, instead of, began to,
how to, keep on, go on (14) Sentences (15) Syntax

Part-1
Chapter 1

Hindi Alphabets: Vowels and Consonants

PRONUNCIATION

VOWELS
(Swar)

अ	आ	इ	ई	उ	ऊ	ए	ऐ
a	aa	e	ee	u	oo	e	ai

ओ	औ	अं	अः
o	au	an	ah

CONSONANTS
(Vyanjan)

क	ख	ग	घ	ङ
ka	Kha	ga	gha	n y
च	छ	ज	झ	ञ
cha	chha	ja	jha	ng
ट	ठ	ड	ढ	ण
ta	tha	da	dha	na
त	थ	द	ध	न
ta	tha	da	dha	na
प	फ	ब	भ	म
pa	pha	ba	bha	ma
य	र	ल	व	
ya	rᵉ	la	va	
श	ष	स	ह	
sha	sha	sa	ha	

क्ष	त्र	ज्ञ
ksha	tra	gya

Note : ण is also written as ण

अ is also written as ण्य

फ़ is also written as झ

In Hindi it is difficult to pronounce consonants without compounding them with vowels. So the consonants include the short sound of A. For instance, क has the sound of K and short A. क् has the sound of K only. Likewise MA means म and M mean म्; TA ट means and T means ट्।

Note: ङ NG and ञ NY are not written independently.

Letters क़, ख़, ग़, ज़ and फ़ have been absorbed in Hindi from Urdu, but these have no corresponding sound in English.

Letters त ta, थ tha, द da, ध dha and न na have soft sound;

ट ta, ठ tha, ड da, ढ dha and ण na have hard sound,

ड़ would be written as r, ढ़ would be written as rh and ँ would be written as an:

Exercise for Reading

प	ट	क	ष	ञ	न	श	ख	ठ
स	फ	र	थ	व	म	भ	ह	छ
ग	ब	ङ	ज	र	न	क्ष	झ	इ

Note :The following letters are very similar :

अ	आ;	इ	ई;	उ	ऊ;	ए	ऐ;	ओ
A	A	I	I	U	U	E	AI	O

औ;	अं	अः	ब	व;	भ	म;
AU	AN	AH	BA	VA	BHA	M A

Chapter 2

Pronunciation: a/अ

I. COMBINATION OF LETTERS

kam	कम	gam	गम	nam	नम
bam	बम	tham	थम	jham	झम
jam	जम	ram	रम	chham	छम
ham	हम	tan	तन	man	मन
dhan	धन	jan	जन	phan	फन
ban	बन	than	ठन	kal	कल
bal	बल	chhal	छल	nal	नल
thal	थल	jal	जल	phal	फल
hal	हल	ab	अब	kab	कब
jab	जब	ghat	घट	nat	नट
tat	तट	rat	रट	hat	हट
kar	कर	nar	नर	mar	मर
ghar	घर	is	इस	us	उस
ras	रस	nas	नस	garam	गरम
naram	नरम	gagan	गगन	gahan	गहन
agar	अगर	magar	मगर	nahar	नहर
shahar	शहर	rasam	रसम	kasam	कसम
kalam	कलम	kamal	कमल	garal	गरल
kharal	खरल	khapat	खपत	rapat	रपट
hamdam	हमदम	hardam	हरदम	kasmas	कसमस
halchal	हलचल	jhamjham	झमझम	marmar	मरमर
garbar	गड़बड़	rahbar	रहबर	rahjan	रहजन
sargam	सरगम				

II. COMBINING THE VOWEL SOUND OF AA/A WITH CONSONANTS

In Hindi one vertical line I is put to blend with the consonant, the long sound of A as pronounced in Ram, grant, father, etc. For instance, NA becomes ना na naa; क ka becomes का ka/kaa; म ma becomes मा ma/maa; laa becomes ल la/laa and so on.

Exercise for mixed

a =अ aa=आ

का	पा	ना	ला	ता	जा	गा	ढा	बा	था
खा	फ़ा	टा	दा	हा	या	शा	रा	झा	घा

work	kaam	काम
name	naam	नाम
gain	Laabh	लाभ
price	daam	दाम
drink	jaam	जाम
news	samachar	समाचार
speed	chal	चाल
beating	maar	मार
defeat	haar	हार
song	gana	गाना
food	khana	खाना
corn	dana	दाना
lock	tala	ताला
brother-in-law	sala	साला
uncle	mama	मामा
copy	khata	खाता
art	kala	कला

angry	krodh	क्रोध
clause	dapha	दफा
profit	laabh	लाभ
death	Mirtu	मृत्यु
dead	mara	मरा
intoxication	nasha	नशा
playing instrument	gada bjana	गद्या बजाना
problem	masla	मसला
ornament	gahna	गहना
to stop	thamna	थमना
to melt	galna	गलना
to die	maarna	मरना
to beat	marna	मारना
to lose	khoya	खोया
to pour	dalna	डालना
to earn	kamana	कमाना
family	pariwar	परिवार
to warm	tapana	तपाना
to bathe	nahana	नहाना

III. COMBINING THE VOWEL SOUNDS
OF इ (I) AND ई

(I) with consonants इ (I) or ई (EE) in Hindi is used independently when the vowel is not combined with any consonant, but when the vowel sound of I or EE is combined with a consonant, a small vertical line with a loop is prefixed, i.e., and a vertical line with a loop is suffixed i.e., for I or EE. For example: हिम (him); चिट (chit); किल(kill)

फील (feel); मीट (meet); शीट (sheet)

Exercise for Reading

| कि | गि | मि | लि | बि | चि | नि | हि | दि | खि |
| ठी | जी | फ़ी | शी | की | पी | री | सी | थी | |

which	kis	किस
that	jis	जिस
lid	lid	लिड
sin	sin	पाप
pin	pin	पिन
day	din	दिन
seat	sit	सिट
rib	rib	रिव
farmer	kisaan	किसान
brain	dimaag	दिमाग
heart	dil	दिल
district	jilaa	जिला
river	nadi	नदी
Himalaya	Himaalay	हिमालय
mood	mijaaz	मिजाज़
liquor	madiraa	मदिरा
thing	cheez	चीज
nail	keel	कील
fish	meen	मछली
scene	seen	सीन
lamp	deep	दीप
backbone	reerh	रीढ़
poor	deen	गरीब
lake	jheel	झील

heat	garmee	गरमी
poor	gareeb	गरीब
rich	ameer	अमीर
cold	sardee	सर्दी
river	nadee	नदी
land	jameen	जमीन
elephant	haathee	हाथी
grandson	naatee	नाती
brain	dimagee	दिमागी
bookish	kitaabee	किताबी
wretch	kameenaa	कमीना
verbal	zabaanee	जबानी
youth	javaanee	जवानी
abuse	gaalee	गाली
sister-in-law	saalee	साली
traveller	raahee	राही
carpet	galeechaa	गलीचा
shirt	kameez	कमीज
wall	deevaar	दीवार
salute	slaamee	सलामी
cloud	baadal	बादल
companions	saathi	साथी
drizzle	rimjhim	रिमझिम
survey	nireekshan	निरीक्षण
lizard	chhipaklee	छिपकली
livelihood	jeevikaa	जीविका
custom	reeti	रीति
under consideration	vichaaraadheen	विचाराधीन

IV. COMBINING THE VOWEL SOUNDS OF उ (U) AND ऊ (OO/U).

But when we blend alphabets with A consonant, we put a small leftward hook, under the consonant. Examples: कु, मु, बु etc.

Similarly, when we use the vowel sound of ऊ (oo/u) independently, we use ऊ (oo/u). But when we blend it with a consonant, we put a downward hook under, the consonanta. Examples: लू, जू, भू etc.

Note: When we blend र (ra) with a consonant, we put the hook in its middle as रू

Exercise for Reading

खु	भु	छु	नु	डु	घु	शु	फु	दु	वु
कू	नू	लू	चू	दू	तू	सू	पू	गू	ठू

Wednesday	budh	बुध
something	kuchh	कुछ
you	tum	तुम
silent	chup	चुप
to break	tootna	टूटना
put	put	पुट
pleased	khush	खुश
to hear	sun	सुन
plunder	loot	लूट
lie	jhoot	झूठ
mute	mook	मूक
miss	chook	चूक
soul	rooh	रूह
little	com	कम

feature	roop	रूप
sun	dhoop	धूप
rose	gulab	गुलाब
old	puranaa	पुराना
collyrium	surmaa	सुरमा
bachelor	kumaar	कुमार
pleasure	khushee	खुशी
miss	kumari	कुमारी
goldsmith	sunar	सुनार
shop	dukaan	दुकान
soap	saabun	साबून
police	pulis	पुलिस
prophet	moosa	मूसा
loss	nuksaan	नुकसान
to smile	muskurana	मुस्कुराना
smile	muskurahat	मुस्कुराहट
dacoit	daakoo	डाकू
chick	roopvatee	रूपवती
bad smell	badboo	बदबू

V. COMBINING THE VOWEL SOUNDS OF ए (E) AND ऐ (AI) WITH CONSONANTS

When we do not blend ए (E) and ऐ (AI) with any consonant, we write them as ए (E) and ऐ (AI), but when we compound them (ए and ऐ) with consonant, we put slanting strokes (` ) for ए ( `) for ऐ

Examples: के, बे, ले for ए (E)

कै, बै, लै for ऐ (AI)

Exercise for Reading

के	चे	टे	ते	पे	ये	गे	जे	दे	ने	हे
थे	धे	फे	बे	वे	टे	झे	खे	घे	छे	भे
खै	छै	ठै	थै	रै	फै	झै	गै	लै	भै	मै
घै	णै	शै	सै	दै	बै	पै	चै	तै		

banana	kelaa	केला
fair	mela	मेला
daughter	batee	बेटी
son	betaa	बेटा
convict	doshi	दोषी
fail	fel	फेल
chicken pox	chechak	चेचक
pennies	dhele	धेले
oilmaker	telee	तेली
galley	galee	गली
turban	murethaa	मुरेठा
bird	panchi	पंछी
bull	bail	बैल
picse	paisaa	पैसा
bag	thailea	थैला
crutch	baisaakhee	बैसाखी
eastern wind	purvaiyaa	पुरवैया
countless	behisaab	बेहिसाब
honorary	avaitanik	अवैतनिक

VI. COMBINING THE VOWEL SOUNDS OF ओ (O) AND औ (AU) WITH CONSONANTS

When we do not blend ओ (O) and औ (AU) with any consonant, we write them as ओ (O) and औ (AU), but when we compound them (ओ and औ) with consonants we put the symbols—(ो) for आ and (ौ) for औ Examples: को, जो, मो, कौ, जौ, मौ

Exercise for Reading

को	चो	टो	तो	पो	गो	जो	डो	वो	मो
खौ	छौ	ठौ	थौ	फौ	घौ	झौ	ढौ	वौ	नौ

corner	konaa	कोना
blouse	cholee	चोली
cap	topee	टोपी
parrot	totaa	तोता
pond	pokhraa	पोखरा
dung	gobar	गोबर
cobbler	mochee	मोची
piece	botee	बोटी
dress	poshak	पोशाक
peacock	mor	मोर
bread	rotee	रोटी
earning	rojee	रोजी
gold	sonaa	सोना
profession	rojgaar	रोजगार
business	kaarobaar	कारोबार
bustle	kolaahal	कोलाहल
hue and cry	kohraam	कोहराम

crow	kauaa	कौआ
dwarf	bauna	बौना
fourth	chauthaa	चौथा
servant	naukar	नौकर
weather	mausam	मौसम
uncle	mausaa	मौसा
barley	jau	जौ
age	daur	दौर
abode	thaur	ठौर
diamond	gauhar	गौहर
woman	aurat	औरत

VII. COMBINING THE VOWEL SOUNDS OF अं (AN) WITH CONSONANTS

When we do not combine अं (AN) with any consonant it is written as अं, but when we compound it with a consonant, we put a small dot or cipher on top of the preceding consonant.

Examples: कं, दं, पं, बं, नं etc.

Exercise for Reading

कंस	kans	दंड	dand	पंत	pant
संत	sant	बंद	band	रंग	rang
भंग	bhang	नंग	nang	संग	sang
पंग	pang				

monkey	bandar	बंदर
coloured	rangeen	रंगीन
poppy	bhaang	भांग
paralysed	pangu	पंगु

pant	pent	पतलून
pink	pink	पिंक
naked	nangaa	नंगा
riot	dangaa	दंगा
ape	langoor	लंगूर
pauper	rank	रंक
paint	paint	पैंट
laundry	laundree	लांडरी
pound	pound	पाउंड
difference	antar	अंतर

Chapter 3
Conjunct Consonants

Now we will let you know how a vowel is combined with a consonant.

Rule I: If two क are combined: क + क = क्क ; ग + ग = ग्ग

Rule II: If क is combined with य : क + य = क्य or कूय as क्या

If त is combined with म : त + म = त्म or तुम as महात्मा

If प is combined with प : प + प = प्प or पूप as अप्पा

If न is combined with न : न + न = न्न or नून as अन्न

If च is combined with छ : च + छ = च्छ or चूछ as अच्छा

If त is combined with थ : त + थ = त्थ or तूथ as कत्था

If ष is combined with ट : ष + ट = ष्ट as शिष्ट

If थ is combined with य : थ + य = थ्य as तथ्य

Exceptions: When we combine क with झ, we retain the vertical line but the curve on the right is halved as क+झ = क्झ

Rule III: When the consonant (which we combine with the succeeding consonant) does not have a vertical line in the end, then the first letter we write as it is and the succeeding letter is joined by putting it below the first as— ट्+ट = ट्ट and ट्+य = ट्य

Rule IV: (i) When र (ra) is the first consonant to be combined, it loses its original form altogether and is denoted by half AR on the top of the second letter as- र+क =र्क; र+म = र्म as अर्क, मर्म

(ii) When र (ra) is the second consonant, we allow it to stand and its sound we denote by a slanting stroke on its left as— प् + र = प्र ; ब + र = ब्र as प्रभात, ब्रज

Note: This rule is applicable when the first consonant has a vertical line.

(iii) When र (ra) is the second letter and its sound is denoted by the symbol, we put in below the consonant as—ट् + र = ट्र ; ड् + र = ड्र

Rule V: Some oddities are there in the forms of conjunct consonants as—

क् + त = क्त kta; त् + त = त्त tta; श + र = श्र shra;
द् + म = द्म dma; द् + य = द्य dya; ह् + म = ह्म hma.

Note: This rule may be ignored as it is not very much in use.

Exercise for Reading

Here are words of English which are in current use in Hindi. Their meaning and connotation in Hindi are the same as in English.

Exercise 1

account	एकाउन्ट	ban	बैन
bill	बिल	appeal	अपील
ball	बॉल	blotting paper	ब्लॉटिंग पेपर
assistant	असिस्टेन्ट	barrister	बैरिस्टर

bomb	बम	bag	बैग
bathroom	बाथरूम	book-post	बुक-पोस्ट
bat	बैट	bicycle	बाईसिकिल
bush shirt	बुशशर्ट	camera	कैमरा
dance	डान्स	goods train	गुड्स ट्रेन
carbon	कार्बन	despatch	डिस्पेच
government	गवर्नमेंट	car	कार
director	डायरेक्टर	guard	गार्ड
card	कार्ड	discount	डिसकाउन्ट छुट
head-master	हेड मास्टर	cash	कैश
district	डिस्ट्रिक्ट जिला	holder	होल्डर
cinema	सिनेमा	doctor	डॉक्टर
income tax	इन्कम टैक्स	class	क्लास
draft	ड्राफ्ट	jail	जेल
club	क्लब	driver	ड्राइवर
judge	जज	college	कॉलेज
engine	इंजिन	junction	जंक्शन
coat	कोट	express	एक्सप्रेस
lamp	लैम्प	coolie	कुली
fast	तेज	late	लेट
compartment	कम्पार्टमेंट	fees	फीस
late-fee	लेट फी	commission	कमीशन
file	फाइल	lemon	लेमन
commissioner	कमिश्नर	fountain pen	फाउन्टेन पेन
luggage	लगेज	copy	कॉपी
gate	गेट	manager	मैनेजर
cup	कप	goal	गोल
map	मैप	market	मार्केट

post box	पोस्ट बॉक्स	set	सेट
master	मास्टर	post card	पोस्ट कार्ड
share	शेयर	money order	मनीआर्डर
postman	पोस्टमैन	stamp	स्टाम्प
packet	पैकेट	post-master	पोस्ट मास्टर
superintendent	सुपरिन्टेन्डेन्ट	pad	पैड
photo	फोटो	table	टेबिल
pant	पैन्ट	picture	पिक्चर
tax	टैक्स	paper	पेपर
press	प्रेस	ticket	टिकट
parcel	पार्सल	principal	प्रिंसिपल
time	टाइम	passenger	यात्री
programme	प्रोग्राम	telephone	टेलिफोन
pen	पेन	racket	रैकेट
tram	ट्राम	pencil	पेन्सिल
radio	रेडियो	type	टाइप
pin	पिन	rail	रेल
wagon	वैगन	plate	प्लेट
rate	रेट	war	युद्ध
platform	प्लेटफार्म	register	रजिस्टर
watch	वाच	post	डाक
rubber	रबर	postal	पोस्टल
order	आर्डर	seat	सीट

Exercise 2

PERSONS

Akbar	अकबर
Jawahar Lal Nehru	जवाहर लाल नेहरू
Satya Narayan Singh	सत्य नारायण सिंह

Abid Ali	आबिद अली
Mohandas Karam Chand Gandhi	मोहनदास करम चंद गांधी
Swarna Singh	स्वर्ण सिंह
Indira Gandhi	इन्दिरा गांधी
Lokmanya Tilak	लोक मान्य तिलक
Dwarka Prasad	द्वारका प्रसाद
Ismat Chugtai	इस्मत चुगताई
Rajgopalachari	राजगोपालाचारी
Pandit Rambhadra	पंडित रामभद्र
Arvind	अरविन्द
Ramkrishna Paramhans	रामकृष्ण परमहंस
Jalaluddin	जलालुद्दीन
Kriplani	कृपलानी
Shyama Prasad Shukla	श्यामा प्रसाद शुक्ला
Gayasuddin	गयासुद्दीन
Kanhaiya Lal	कन्हैया लाल
Anantshayanam Ayyangar	अनंत शयनम अय्यंगर
Vikramaditya	विक्रमादित्य
Chandragupta	चन्द्रगुप्त
Krishna Aiyyar	कृष्ण अय्यर
Gautam Buddha	गौतम बुद्ध
Samrat Ashoka	सम्राट अशोक
Radhaswami	राधास्वामी
Uma Shankar Dikshit	उमा शंकर दीक्षित
Mirza Ghalib	मिर्ज़ा ग़ालिब
Rajendra Prasad	राजेन्द्र प्रसाद
Kutubuddin	कुतुबुद्दीन
Radhakrishnan	राधाकृष्णन

Maharana Pratap	महाराणा प्रताप
Krishna Menon	कृष्ण मेनन
Zakir Husain	ज़ाकिर हुसैन
Morarji Desai	मोरारजी देसाई
Ustad Vilayat Khan	उस्ताद विलायत खां
Lal Bahadur Shastri	लाल बहादुर शास्त्री
Vishwanathan	विश्वनाथन
Gajendragadkar	गजेन्द्रगड़कर
Firaq Gorakhpuri	फिराक गोरखपुरी
Ashok Kumar	अशोक कुमार
Vidya Chandra	विद्याचंद्र
Venkatraman	वेंकटरमन
Maharshi Dayanand	महर्षि दयानंद
Nityanand Chaudhari	नित्यानंद चौधरी
Devvrat	देवव्रत
Chittaranjan Das	चित्तरंजन दास
Swami Vivekanand	स्वामी विवेकानंद
Sachchidanand	सच्चिदानंद
Shyama Prasad Mukherji	श्यामा प्रसाद मुखर्जी
Ramtirth	रामतीर्थ
Ranchhod Das	रणछोड़ दास
Hidayatulla	हिदायतुल्ला

STATES

Nagaland	नागालैंड	Tamilnadu	तमिलनाडु
Uttar Pradesh	उत्तर प्रदेश	Bihar	बिहार
Kerala	केरल	Rajasthan	राजस्थान

Assam	असम	Mysore	मैसूर
Punjab	पंजाब	Bengal	बंगाल
Maharashtra	महाराष्ट्र	Jammu and	जम्मू और
		Kashmir	कश्मीर
Orrisa	उड़ीसा	Gujarat	गुजरात
Andhra	आंध्र	Madhya Pradesh	मध्य प्रदेश

CITIES

Chandigarh	चण्डीगढ़	Delhi	दिल्ली
Mumbai	मुम्बई	kolkata	कोलकात्ता
Hyderabad	हैदराबाद	Agra	आगरा
Chennai	चेन्नई	Jamshedpur	जमशेदपुर
Varanasi	वाराणसी	Banaras	बनारस
Patna	पटना	Banglaur	बंगलोर
Kanpur	कानपुर	Ranchi	रांची
Amritsar	अमृतसर	Nagpur	नागपुर
Jabalpur	जबलपुर	Mathura	मथुरा
Ahmedabad	अहमदाबाद	Ujjain	उज्जैन
Bikaner	बीकानेर	Ilahabad	इलाहाबाद
Lucknow	लखनऊ	Azamgarh	आजमगढ़

MOUNTAINS

Himalaya	हिमालय	Vindhya	विन्धया
Aravalee	अरावली	Neelgiri	नीलगिरी
Parsnath	पारसनाथ	Sumeru	सुमेरू

RIVERS

| Ganga | गंगा | Godavaree | गोदावरी |
| Son | सोन | Yamuna | यमुना |

Gomatee	गोमती	Jhelam	झेलम
Krishna	कृष्णा	Sindhu	सिन्धु
Chenab	चेनाव	Kaveri	कावेरी
Brahmputra	ब्रह्मपुत्र	Vyas	व्यास
Narmada	नर्मदा	Ravi	रावी
Chambal	चम्बल		

HILL STATIONS

Shimla	शिमला	Nainital	नैनीताल
Gulmarg	गुलमर्ग	Mussouri	मसूरी
Darjeeling	दार्जिलिंग	Pahalgam	पहलगाम

We are introducing now the letters which have very much similarity in their written forms. They are as follows:

(i)   भ (bha) and म (ma)

(ii) ब (ba) and व (va)

(iii) ध (dha) and घ(gha)

(iv) स (sa) and प (pa)

Now read the following:

1.	Mohan is my brother.	Mohan mera bhaee hai	मोहन मेरा भाई है
2.	Radha is his/ her mother.	Radha uskee mata hai	राधा उसकी माता है
3.	I have a sister.	Meri ek bahan hai	मेरी एक बहन है
4.	He is a thief	Wah chor hai	वह चोर है
5.	The earth is vast.	Dhartee vishal hai	धरती विशाल है
6.	Grass is green	Ghas haree hai	घास हरी है
7.	Radhika is sixteen	Radhika soleh ke hai	राधिका सोलह की है
8.	I need fifty paise/pice	Mujhe pachas paise chahiye	मुझे पचास पैसे चाहिए

9.	innocent	Bhola bhala	भोला-भाला
10.	sweet	Madhur	मधुर
11.	non culprit	begunah	बेगुनाह
12.	salary	vetan	वेतन
13.	profession	dhandha	धंधा
14.	horseman	ghursavar	घुड़सवार

Chapter 4
Exercise for Reading

LETTERS IN COMPOUND WORDS

1.	प	ष	छ	ध	घ	ब	व	श	स	क्ष
	न	ण	ण	फ	अं	ज्ञ	ग	च	त	अ
	ङ	ड	ड़	ढ	ढ़	ठ	ट	ब	व	आ
	इ	ई	औ	ए	ओ					

kam	कम		madan	मदन
than	थन		daman	दमन
nath	नथ		sahar	सहर
mar	मर		hasar	हसर
ram	रम		gahan	गहन
man	मन		kapat	कपट
nam	नम		naram	नरम
ras	रस		maran	मरन
sar	सर		rasam	रसम
ghat	घट		saram	सरम
bas	बस		khasam	खसम
sab	सब		jhapat	झपट
tar	तर		agar	अगर

rat	रत	nahar	नहर
eekh	ईख	hamdam	हमदम
ek	एक	rahbar	रहबर
ot	ओट	halchal	हलचल
lat	लट	sarpat	सरपट
tal	टल	marmar	मरमर
aib	ऐब	kasmas	कसमस
kalam	कलम	sargam	सरगम
kamal	कमल	rahjan	रहजन
garbar	गड़बड़	pahalwaanee	पहलवानी
jhamjham	झमझम	chahalkadmee	चहलकदमी
kaam	काम	jeevikaa	जीविका
kamaa	कमा	nireekshan	निरीक्षण
Ram	राम	chhipkilee	छिपकली
maraa	मरा	vichaarsheel	विचारशील
maaree	मारी	bu	बु
kaalaa	काला	budh	बुध
kalaa	कला	ku	कु
kaal	काल	kul	कुल
kalam	कलम	kumar	कुमार
kamal	कमल	khumaree	खुमारी
kamaal	कमाल	kulpati	कुलपति
salaam	सलाम	gulaabee	गुलाबी
mashaal	मशाल	gulshan	गुलशन
kapaat	कपाट	anjuman	अंजुमन
jhamaajham	झमाझम	bulbul	बुलबुल
khachaakhach	खचाखच	saabundaanee	साबुनदानी
labaalab	लबालब	gulbadan	गुलबदन

haraarat	हरारत	moo	मू
nafaasat	नफासत	mook	मूक
sharaafat	शराफत	roohafzaa	रूहअफज़ा
kasmasaahat	कसमसाहट	jansamooh	जनसमूह
chhatpataahat	छटपटाहट	poorn	पूर्ण
anban	अनबन	sooksmataa	सूक्ष्मता
zalzalaa	ज़लज़ला	koop	कूप
karaamaat	करामात	soochnaa	सूचना
din	दिन	sooee	सूई
dinaank	दिनांक	tootiya	तूतिया
dimaagdaar	दिमागदार	kaanoongo	कानूनगो
dariyaadil	दरियादिल	goodhaakshar	गूढ़ाक्षर
deen	दीन	shoonya	शून्य
deendayaal	दीनदयाल	anuraag	अनुराग
aasmaanee	आसमानी	bhoomi	भूमि
dudaaru	दूधारू	aadhaarbhoot	आधारभूत
		pustikaa	पुस्तिका
gairhajiree	गैरहाज़िरी	soochee	सूची
avahelnaa	अवहेलना	choolha	चूल्हा
nairaashya	नैराश्य	saaboodaanaa	साबूदाना
supaaree	सुपारी	avaidh	अवैध
vimukh	विमुख	peshgee	पेशगी
anuvaadit	अनुवादित	paigaam	पैगाम
anukool	अनुकूल	paidal	पैदल
moolyaanusaar	मूल्यानुसार	vidheyak	विधेयक
ke	के	vivechan	विवेचन
kelaa	केला	haijaa	हैजा
belee	बेली	ro	रो

dhele	धेले	rok	रोक
medhaavee	मेधावी	rokaa	रोका
rotee	रोटी	kurukshetra	कुरुक्षेत्र
jokhim	जोखिम	meharbaanee	मेहरबानी
joru	पटनी	Ahatia	आतिथ्य
toke	टोके	watan	वतन
hovaidaa	होवेदा	kaabile-taareef	प्रशसां पूर्ण
goraiyaa	गोरैया	bai	बै
trilochan	त्रिलोचन	bail	बैल
aarogya	आरोग्य	sailaab	सैलाब
oshadhi	दवाई	khairkhaahee	खैरखाही
kolahalpoorn	कोलाहलपूर्ण	gairat	गैरत
kau	कौ	maidaan	मैदान
kauaa	कौआ	zuvaidaa	जुवैदा
kaun	कौन	baisaakh	बैसाख
baunee	बौनी	daure	दौरे
sailaanee	सैलानी	choksee	चौकसी
daitya	दैत्य	faujdaraee	फौजदारी
vairaagee	वैरागी	chaupaal	चौपाल
Nainital	नैनीताल	chaukeedaar	चौकीदार
kan	कान	kyaa	क्या
kans	कंस	mahatma	महात्मा
kanghaa	कंघा	appaa	अप्पा
bandee	बंदी	anna	अन्न
phande	फंदे	achchhaa	अच्छा
kandil	कंदिल	kattha	कत्था
bhangur	भंगुर	tathya	तथ्य

langoor	लंगूर	ark	अर्क
pendaa	पेंदा	marm	मर्म
paint	पैंट	prabhaa	प्रभा
paund	पॉउंड	traam	ट्राम
pinki	पिंकी	draam	ड्राम

A CHART TO ENABLE YOU COMBINE THE MATRAS WITH CONSONANTS

क ka	म ma	ल la	प pa	न na
का kaa	मा maa	ला laa	पा paa	ना naa
कि ki	मि mi	लि li	पि pi	नि ni
की kee	मी mee	ली lee	पी pee	नी nee
कु ku	मु mu	लु lu	पु pu	नु nu
कू koo	मू moo	लू loo	पू poo	नू noo
के ke	मे me	ले le	पे pe	ने nai
कै kai	मै mai	लै lai	पै pai	नै nai
को ko	मो mo	लो lo	पो po	नो no
कौ kau	मौ mau	लौ lau	पौ pau	नौ nau
कं kan	मं man	लं lan	पं pan	नं·nan
कः kah	मः mah	लः lah	पः pah	नः nah

Part-2
Chapter 1

Parts of Human Body

Ankle	takhnaa(M)	टखना
Arm	baanh(F) (Sin.)	बांह
Armpit	bagal (F) (Sin.)	बगल

Back	peeth (F) (Sin.)	पीठ
Beard	daarhee (F) (Sin.)	दाढ़ी
Belly	pat (M) (Sin & Plu.)	पेट
Blood	khoon (M) (Sin. & Plu.)	खून
Body	shareer (M) (Sin. & Plu.)	शरीर
Bosom	chati (M) (Sin. & Plu.)	छाती
Brain	dimaag (M) (Sin. & Plu.)	दिमाग
Breast	stan (M) (Sin. & Plu.) (woman's)	स्तन .
Cheek	gaal (M) (Sin. & Plu.)	गाल
Chest	chhaatee (M) (Sin. & Plu.)	छाती
Chin	thodee (M) (Sin. & Plu.)	ठोड़ी
Ear	kaan (M) (Sin. & Plu.)	कान
Elbow	kuhnee (M) (Sin.)	कुहनी
Eye	aankh (M) (Sin.)	आँख
Eyeball	putlee (M) (Sin.)	पुतली
Eyebrow	baroni (M) (Sin.)	बरौनी
Eyelash	palak (M) (Sin.)	पलक
Eyelid	palak (M) (Sin.)	पलक
Face	chehraa (M) (Sin.)	चेहरा
Finger	angulee (M) (Sin.)	अंगुली
Fist	mutthee (M) (Sin.)	मुट्ठी
Flesh	gosht (M) (Sin.)	गोश्त
Foot	pair (M) (Sin.)	पैर
Forehead	maathaa (M) (Sin.)	माथा
Gum	masuraa (M) (Sin.)	मसूड़ा
Hand	haath (M) (Sin. & Plu.)	हाथ
Hair	baal (M) (Sin. & Plu.)	बाल
Head	sir (M) (Sin. & Plu.)	सिर

Heart	dil(M) (Sin. & Plu.)	दिल
Heel	edee (M) (Sin.)	एड़ी
Hip	koolhaa (M) (Sin.)	कूल्हा
Knee	ghutnaa (M) (Sin.)	घुटना
Kidney	gurdaa (M) (Sin.)	गुरदा
Leg	taang (M) (Sin.)	टांग
Lip	honth (M) (Sin. & Plu.)	होंठ
Liver	jigar (M) (Sin. & Plu.)	जिगर
Lung	phephraa (M) (Sin.)	फेफड़ा
Moustache	moonchh (M) (Sin.)	मूंछ
Mouth	munh (M) (Sin. & Plu.)	मुंह
Nail	naakhun (M) (Sin. & Plu.)	नाखून
Neck	gardan (M) (Sin. & Plu.)	गर्दन
Nose	naak (M) (Sin. & Plu.)	नाक
Palm	hathelee (M) (Sin. & Plu.)	हथेली
Shoulder	kandhaa (M) (Sin.)	कंधा
Skin	chamree (M) (Skin.)	चमड़ी
Skull	khopree (M) (Sin.)	खोपड़ी
Spine	readh (M) (Sin.)	रीढ़
Sole	talwaa(M) (Sin.)	तलवा
Stomach	pet (M) (Sin. & Plu.)	पेट
Teeth	daant (M) (Plu.)	दांत
Thigh	jaangh (M) (Sin.)	जांघ
Throat	galaa (M) (Sin.)	गला
Thumb	angoothaa (M) (Sin.)	अंगूठा
Vein	nas (M) (Sin.)	नस
Waist	kamar (M) (Sin.)	कमर
Wrist	kalaee (M) (Sin.)	कलाई

* (M) denotes male: (F) denotes female, (Sin.) denotes singular: (Plu.) denotes plural.

Chapter 2
Animals, Birds, Insects

I ANIMALS ON THE EARTH

Animal	jaanwar (M)	जानवर
Bull	saandh (M)	सांड़
Bullock	bail (M)	बैल
Buffalo	bhains (F), bhainsaa (M)	भैंस, भैंसा
Bitch	kutiyaa (F)	कुतिया
Calf	bachhraa(M)	बछड़ा
Calf	bachhiyaa (F)	बछिया
Cat	billee (F)	बिल्ली
Chamelion	girgit (M)	गिरगिट
Camel	oont (M), oontnee (F)	ऊंट, ऊंटनी
Cow	gaay (F)	गाय
Deer	hiran (M)	हिरन
Dog	kuttaa (M)	कुत्ता
Donkey	gadhaa (M)	गधा
Elephant	haathee (M)	हाथी
Fox	lomree (F)	लोमड़ी
Goat	bakraa (M)	बकरा
Hare	khargosh (M)	खरगोश
Heifer	osar (F)	ओसर
Horse	ghoraa (M)	घोड़ा
Hound	shikaaree kutta (M)	शिकारी कुंत्ता
Jackal	geedar (M)	गीदड़
Lamb	memnaa (M)	मेमना
Leopard	cheetaa (M)	चीता

Lion	sher (M)	शेर
Lioness	shernee (F)	शेरनी
Mare	ghoree (F)	घोड़ी
Mongoose	newlaa (M)	नेवला
Monkey	bandar (M)	बंदर
Mouse	chuhaa (M)	चूहा
Mule	khachchar (M)	खच्चर
Pig	suvar (M)	सुअर
Pup	**pillaa (M)**	**पिल्ला**
Python	ajgar (M)	अजगर
Ram	maindhaa (M)	मैंढ़ा
Rhinoceros	gaindaa (M)	गैंड़ा
Sheep	bher (F)	भेड़
Skunk	chhachhundar (M)	छछुन्दर
Snake	saanp (M)	सांप
Squirrel	gilharee (F)	गिलहरी
Stag	baarahsingaa (M)	बारहसिंगा
Swine	suvar (M)	सुअर
Tiger	baagh (M)	बाघ
Tigress	baaghin (F)	बाघिन
Tom	bilaav (M)	बिलाव
Wolf	bheriyaa (F)	भेड़िया

II BIRDS

Bat	chamgaadad (M)	चमगादड़
Bird	pakshee (M)	पक्षी
Cock	murgaa (M)	मुर्गा
Crane	saaras (M)	सारस
Crow	kauvaa (M)	कौआ

Cuckoo	koyal (F)	कोयल
Dove	kameree (F)	कमेड़ी
Duck	battakh (F)	बत्तख
Hen	murgee (F)	मुर्गी
Kite	cheel (F)	चील
Nightingale	bulbul (F)	बुलबुल
Partridge	teetar (M)	तीतर
Parrot	totaa (M)	तोता
Peacock	mor (M)	मोर
Pigeon	kabootar (M)	कबूतर
Sparrow	goraiyaa (F)	गौरैया
Swan	hans (M)	हंस
Vulture	geedh (M)	गिद्ध
Owl	ulloo (M)	उल्लू

III ANIMALS IN THE WATER

Crab	kekraa (M)	केकड़ा
Crocodile	magar (M)	मगर
Fish	machhlee (F)	मछली
Leech	jonk (M)	जोंक
Tortoise	kachhuvaa (M)	कछुआ

IV INSECTS

Ant	cheetee (F)	चींटी
Bee	madhumakkhee (F)	मधुमक्खी
Bug	khatmal (M)	खटमल
Butterfly	titlee (F)	तितली
Fly	makkhee (F)	मक्खी
Frog	mendhak (M)	मेंढक

Germs	keetaanu (M)	कीटाणु
Glowworm	jugnoo (M)	जुगनू
Insect	keeraa (M)	कीड़ा
Lizard	chhipkalee (F)	छिपकली
Locust	tiddee (F)	टिड्डी
Mosquito	machchhar (M)	मच्छर
Scorpion	bichchhoo (F)	बिच्छू
Spider	makree (F)	मकड़ी
Snail	ghongha (M)	घोंघा
Wasp	tataiyaa (M)	ततैया

* (M) denotes male: (F) denotes female.

Chapter 3

Foodstuff, Vegetables, Fruits, Flowers, Spices, Grains, etc.

I FOODSTUFF

Beef	maans (Gaay kaa) (M)	गाय का मांस
Bread	roti (F)	रोटी
Breakfast	naashtaa (M)	नाश्ता
Buttermilk	chhachh (F)	छाछ
Butter	makkhan (M)	मक्खन
Chapaatee	roti (F)	रोटी
Cheese	paneer (M)	पनीर
Chicken	murgee (F)	मुर्गी
Coffee	caufee (F)	कॉफी
Corn	makka (M)	मक्का
Curd	dahee (M)	दही

Curry	karhee (F)	कढ़ी
Dinner	raat kaa khaanaa (M)	रात का खाना
Egg	andaa (M)	अंडा
Flour	aattaa (M)	आटा
Gram	chanaa (M)	चना
Honey	shahad (M)	शहद
Jaggery	gur (M)	गुड़
Lunch	dopahar kaa khaanaa (M)	दोपहर का खाना
Meal	bhojan (M)	भोजन
Meat	maans (M)	मांस
Milk	doodh (M)	दूध
Mutton	maans (bakre kaa) (M)	मांस (बकरे का)
Oil	tel (M)	तेल
Pickle	achaar (M)	अचार
Pork	maans (sauvar kaa) (M)	मांस (सुअर का)
Pulse	daal (F)	दाल
Rice	chaawal (M)	चावल
Salt	namak (M)	नमक
Soup	jhol	झोल
Sugar	cheenee (F)	चीनी
Sweets	mithaaee (F)	मिठाई
Tea	chaay (F)	चाय
Venison	maans (hiran kaa) (M)	मांस (हिरन का)
Vinegar	sirkaa (M)	सिरका
Wheat	gehoon (M)	गेंहू
Wine	sharaab (F)	शराब

II VEGETABLES

Beans	sem (F)	सेम
Brinjal	baigan (M)	बैंगन
Carrot	gagar (F)	गाजर
Cauliflower	phol gobhee (F)	फुल गोभी
Cabbage	band gobhee (F)	बन्द गोभी
Coriander	dhaniyaa (M)	धनिया
Cucumber	kheeraa (M)	खीरा
Garlic	lahsun (M)	लहसुन
Lemon	neeboo (M)	नीबू
Mint	pudeenaa (M)	पोदीना
Okra	bhindee (F)	भिंडी
Onion	pyaaz (F)	प्याज
Peas	matar (F)	मटर
Pepper	mirch (F)	मिर्च
Potato	aalu	आलू
Pumpkin	kaddoo (M)	कद्दू
Radish	moolee (M)	मूली
Spinach	paalak (M)	पालक
Tomato	tamaatar (M)	टमाटर
Turnip	shalgam (F)	शलगम

III FRUITS

Almond	baadaam (M)	बादाम
Apple	seb (M)	सेब
Apricot	khumaanee (F)	खुमानी
Banana	kelaa (M)	केला
Blackberry	jaamun (M)	जामुन

Chestnut	akhrot (M)	अखरोट
Coconut	naariyal (M)	नारियल
Currant	kishmish (M)	किशमिश
Custard apple	shareefaa (M)	शरीफा
Date	khajoor (M)	खजूर
Fig	anjeer (F)	अंजीर
Guava	amrood (M)	अमरूद
Groundnut	moongphalee (F)	मूंगफली
Jackfruit	kathal (M)	कटहल
Mango	aam (M)	आम
Muskmelon	kharboojaa (M)	खरबूजा
Orange	naarangee (F)	नारंगी
Papaya	papeetaa (M)	पपीता
Pear	naaspaatee (M)	नाशपाती
Pineapple	anannaas (M)	अनन्नास
Pistachio	pistaa (M)	पिस्ता
Pomegranate	anaar (M)	अनार
Raisin	munakka (M)	मुनक्का
Sugarcane	ganna (M)	गन्ना
Sweet potato	shakarkand (M)	शकरकंद
Tamarind	imlee (F)	इमली
Watermelon	tarbooj (M)	तरबूज

IV FLOWERS

Acacla	babool	बबूल
Balsam	gulmehndee	गुलमेंहदी
Chrysanthemum	guldaaudee	गुलदाऊदी
Daisy	gulbahaar	गुलबहार

Jasmine	chamelee	चमेली
Lilac	bakaaen	बकाइन
Lily	kamalinee	कमलिनी
Lotus	kamal	कमल
Magnolia	champaa	चम्पा
Marigold	gendaa	गेंदा
Mushroom	kukurmuttaa	कुकरमुत्ता
Myrtle	mehandee	मेंहदी
Narcissus	nargis	नरगिस
Pandanus	ketkee	केतकी
Rose	gulaab	गुलाब

V SPICES AND CONDIMENTS

Alum	phitkaree	फिटकरी
Aniseed	saunph	सौंफ
Asafoetida	heeng	हींग
Black pepper	kaalee mirch	काली मिर्च
Camphor	kapoor	कपूर
Cardamom	ilaaychee	इलायची
Cassia	tejpaat	तेजपात
Chilli	mirchaa	मिर्चा
Cinnamon	daalcheenee	दालचीनी
Cloves	lavang	लवंग
Cubeb	kabaabcheenee	कबाब चीनी
Cuminseed	jeeraa	जीरा
Dry ginger	sonth	सोंठ
Fenugreek	methee	मेथी
Garlic	lahsun	लहसुन

Ginger	adrakh	अदरख
King's cumin	ajvaain	अजवाइन
Mace	jaavitree	जावित्री
Mint	pudinaa	पुदीना
Musk	kastooree	कस्तूरी
Mustard	raaee	सरसों
Nutmeg	jaayphal	जायफल
Parsley	ajmodaa	अजमोदा
Saffron	keshar	केशर
Spices	masaale	मसाले
Turmeric	haldee	हल्दी

VI GRAINS

Beaten paddy	chivraa	चिवड़ा
Blackgram	urad	उड़द
Grain	ann	अन्न
Gram	chanaa	चना
Kidney-beans	moong	मूंग
Lentil	masoor	मसूर
Mash	daliyaa	दलिया
Millet	baajraa	बाजरा
Oat	jaee	जई
Paddy	post	पोस्त
Rice	chaawal	चावल
Sesame	til	तिल
Wheat	gehoon	गेहूं

Chapter-4

House & its parts, Domestic articles, Weights & Measures, Coins & Fractions, Dress, Makeup, Reading & Writing and Relationships

1. HOUSE & ITS PARTS

Abattoir	kasaeekhaanaa	कसाईखाना
Ante-chamber	dyodhee	चौखटा
Arch	mehraab	मेहराब
Attic	ataaree	अटारी
Bar	chhar	छड़
Barrack	bairak	बैरक
Bathroom	snaangrih	स्नानगृह
Battlement	munder	मुंडेर
Beam	dharan	धरन
Bracket	konyaa	कोना
Brick	eent	ईंट
Building	imaarat	इमारत
Bungalow	banglaa	बंगला
Chain	janjeer	जंजीर
Chimney	dhuankash	धुआंकश
Church	girjaaghar	गिरजाघर
Cloister	math	मठ
Cornice	kaarnis	कारनिस
College	caalej	कॉलेज
Corridor	galiayara	गलियारा
Cottage	jhonpree	झोपड़ी

English	Transliteration	Hindi
Courtyard	aangan	आंगन
Dais	machaan	मचान
Door	darwaajaa	दरवाजा
Doorframe	chaukhat	चौखट
Doorstep	dehleej	देहलीज
Drain	naabdaan	नाबदान
Eaves	oree	ओरी
Factory	kaarkhaanaa	कारखाना
Floor	farsh	फर्श
Fort	kilaa	किला
Foundation	neenv	नींव
Fountain	phauvaaraa	फौवारा
Gallery	galiyaaraa	गलियारा
Getter	parnaalaa	परनाला
Granary	khalihaan	खलिहान
Gurdwara	gurudvara	गुरुद्वारा
Hearth	angeethee	अंगीठी
Hospital	aspataal	अस्पताल
House	ghar	घर
Kitchen	resoeeghar	रसोईघर
Library	pustakaalay	पुस्तकालय
Lunatic asylum	paagalkhaanaa	पागलखाना
Mosque	masjid	मस्जिद
Niche	aalaa	आला
Orphanage	anaathaalay	अनाथालय
Palace	mahal	महल
Peephole	jharokhaa	झरोखा
Peg	khuntee	खूंटी

Plaster	palastar	पलस्तर
Platform	chabutaraa	चबूतरा
Plinth	band	बन्द
Portico	barsaatee	बरसाती
Rafter	shahteer	शहतीर
Railing	dandharaa	डंडहरा
Roof	chhat	छत
Room	kamraa	कमरा
School	paathshaalaa	पाठशाला
Shed	chhappar	छप्पर
Stair	seedhee	सीढ़ी
Steeple	meenaar	मीनार
Stone	patthar	पत्थर
Storey	khand	खण्ड
Temple	mandir	मंदिर
Tile	khaprail	खपरैल
Urinal	peshaabghar	पेशाबघर
Verandah	baramdaa	बरामदा
Window	khirkee	खिड़की

II DOMESTIC ARTICLES

Almirah	almaaree	अलमारी
Basket	tokaree	टोकरी
Bed	chaarpaaee	चारपाई
Bed	palang	पलंग
Bedsheet	chaadar	चादर
Bench	bench	बेंच
Bobbin	antee	अंटी

Bolster	masnad	मसनद
Bottle	botal	बोतल
Box	dibbaa	डिब्बा
Bracket	divaalgeer	दिवालगीर
Brush	burush	ब्रुश
Bucket	baaltee	बाल्टी
Candle	mombattee	मोमबत्ती
Canister	kanastar	कनस्तर
Casket	singaardan	सिंगारदान
Cauldron	karaaha	कड़ाह
Censer	dhoopdaanee	धूपदानी
Chain	sikree	सिकड़ी
Chair	kursee	कुरसी
Chandelier	phaanoos	फानूस
Churner	mathnee	मथनी
Comb	kanghee	कंघी
Dish	rakaabee	रकाबी
Flour-mill	chakkee	चक्की
Fork	konchnee	कोंचनी
Funnel	keep	कीप
Grate	jhanjhree	झंझरी
Hubble-bubble	hukkaa	हुक्का
Inkpot	davaat	दवात
Jar	gagraa	गगरा
Jug	suraahee	सुराही
Key	chaabhee	चाभी
Ladle	karchhee	करछी
Lid	dhaknaa	ढकना

Lock	taalaa	ताला
Lotah	lotaa	लोटा
Mat	chataaee	चटाई
Match	diyaasalaaee	दियासलाई
Mirror	darpan	शीशा
Mortar	okhlee	ओखली
Needle	suee	सुई
Oven	tandoor	तंदूर
Palanquin	paalkee	पालकी
Pastry board	chaklaa	चकला
Pen	lekhnee	लेखनी
Pestle	lorhaa	लोढ़ा
Phial	sheeshee	शीशी
Pillow	takiyaa	तकिया
Pincers	sanrsee	संड़सी
Plate	thaalee	थाली
Pot	bartan	बर्तन
Probe	salaaee	सलाई
Rope	rassaa	रस्सा
Safe	tijoree	तिजोरी
Sieve	chalnee	छलनी
Soap	saabun	साबुन
Sack	boraa	बोरा
Spittoon	peekdaan	पीकदान
Spoons	chamchaa	चमचा
Sticks	chharee	छड़ी
Stool	tipaaee	तिपाई
Stoves	choolhaa	चूल्हा

String	rassee	रस्सी
Table	mej	मेज़
Thimble	angustaanaa	अंगुस्ताना
Tongs	chimtaa	चिमटा
Tray	kishtee	किश्ती
Tumbler	gilaas	गिलास
Umbrella	chhaataa	छाता
Wire	taar	तार
Wick	battee	बत्ती

III. WEIGHTS & MEASURES

Balance	taraaju	तराजू
Beam	dandee	डंडी
Counterpoise	dharaa	धड़ा
Dozen	darzan	दर्जन
Foot	phut	फुट
Gram	graam	ग्राम
Inch	inch	इंच
Kilogram	kilograam	किलोग्राम
Litre	litar	लिटर
Metre	meetar	मीटर
Measure	maap	माप
Mile	meel	मील
Ounce	auns	औंस
Pan	palraa	पलड़ा
Pound	paund	पौंड
Quire	dastaa	दस्ता
Ream	reem	रीम

Scale	skel	स्केल
Weight	wajan	वजन
Yard	gaj	गज

IV. COINS & FRACTIONS

Half	aadhaa	आधा
One and a half	derha	डेढ़
One and a quarter	savaa	सवा
One and three	paune do	पौने दो
One-fourth	ek chauthaaee	एक चौथाई
One-third	ek tihaaee	एक तिहाई
Pice	paisaa	पैसा
Rupee	rupayaa	रुपया
Two and a half	dhaaee	ढाई
Three-fourth	teen chauthaaee	तीन चौथाई
To add	jornaa	जोड़ना
To divide	bhaag denaa	भाग देना
To multiply	gunaa karnaa	गुणा करना
To subtract	ghataanaa	घटाना

V. DRESS

Belt	kamarband	कमरबंद
Blanket	kambal	कम्बल
Brocade	kimkhaab	किमखाब
Bedsheet	chaadar	चादर
Bodice	angiyaa	अंगिया
Border	kinaaraa	किनारा
Button	batan	बटन
Boots	joota	जूता

Bra	brejiyar	ब्रैज़ियर
Coat	kot	कोट
Chintz	chheent	छींट
Cotton	ruee	रुई
Cloth	kapraa	कपड़ा
Cashmira	kashmeeraa	कश्मीरा
Canvas	kirmich	किरमिच
Cushion	gaddaa	गद्दा
Cap	topee	टोपी
Cloak	labaadaa	लबादा
Diaper Brocade	kaamdaanee	कामदानी
Darning	rafoo	रफू
Damask	jaamdaanee	जामदानी
Flannel	phalaalain	फलालैन
Gloves	dastaanaa	दस्ताना
Hat	top	टोप
Half-pant	jaanghiyaa	जांघिया
Handkerchief	roomaal	रूमाल
Jacket	phatuhee	फतुही
Lining	astar	अस्तर
Lace	pattaa	पट्टा
Longcloth	latthaa	लट्ठा
Lappet	chikan	चिकन
Muffler	gulooband	गुलूबंद
Napkin	angochhaa	अंगोछा
Pocket	jeb	जेब
Pant	paint	पैंट

Petticoat	saayaa	साया
Quilt	lihaaf	लिहाफ
Scarf	dupattaa	दुपट्टा
Sleeve	aasteen	आस्तीन
Shirt	kameej	कमीज
Shawl	dushaala	दुशाला
Stocking	mojaa	मोजा
Stitching	silaaee	सिलाई
Silk	resham	रेशम
Satin	saatan	साटन
Serge	saraj	सर्ज
Thread	dhaagaa	धागा
Tunic	angarkhaa	अंगरखा
Towel	tauliyaa	तौलिया
Trousers	paayjaamaa	पायजामा
Tape	pheeta	फीता
Turban	pagree	पगड़ी
Turban	saaphaa	साफा
Veil	ghoonghat	घूंघट
Velvet	makhmal	मखमल
Wool	oon	ऊन
Waistcoat	vaaskat	वास्कट
Yarn	soot	सूत

VI A MAKE-UP, JEWELS AND ORNAMENTS

Anklet	painjnee	पैंजनी
Armlet	baajooband	बाजूबंद
Bangle	karaa, chooree	कड़ा, चूड़ी

Bracelet	kangan	कंगन
Brooch	kaanta (saare kaa)	कांटा (साड़ी का)
Chain	sikree	सिकड़ी
Chignon	jooraa	जूड़ा
Clip	chimtee	चिमटी
Collyrium	kaajal	काजल
Collyrium	surmaa	सुरमा
Ear-ring	karnphool	कर्णफूल
Ear-stud	kaan kaa gahanaa	गहना (कान का)
Hairpin	kaantaa (baal kaa)	काँटा(बाल का)
Head locket	maang teekaa	मांग टीका
Locket	latkan	लटकन
Mehndee	menhdee	मेंहदी
Mother of pearl	motee kee seep	मोती की सीप
Necklet	hansulee	हँसली
Necklace	haar	हार
Nose-pin	keel (naak kee)	कील (नाक की)
Nose-ring	nathnee	नथनी
Pendant	lolak	लोलक
Powder	paaudar	पाउडर
Ring	angoothee	अँगूठी
Scent	itra	इत्र
Shampoo	shaimpoo	शैम्पू
Snow	sno	स्नो
Soap	saabun	साबुन
Tiara	mukut	मुकुट
Watch	gharee	घड़ी
Wristlet	toraa	तोड़ा

Wreath	mala	माला
Agate	sulemaanee	सुलेमानी
Cat's eye	lahsuniyaan	लहसुनिया
Coral	moongaa	मूंगा
Emerald	pannaa	पन्ना
Gems	javaaharaat	जवाहरात
Opal	polkee	पोलकी
Pearl	motee	मोती
Pebble	billaur	बिल्लौर
Ruby	maanik	मानिक
Sapphire	neelam	नीलम्
Topaz	pukhraaj	पुखराज
Turquoise	feerojaa	फीरोजा
Zircon	gomedak	गोमेदक

VII WRITING & READING

Blotting paper	syaheechus	स्याहीचूस
Book	kitaab	किताब
Calling bell	ghantee	घंटी
Card	kaard	कार्ड
Clip	chimtee	चिमटी
Chalk	khariyaa	खड़िया
Cork	kaag	काग
Crayon	khariyaa pencil	खड़िया पेंसिल
Daily paper	dainik patra	दैनिक पत्र
Dividers	parkaar	परकार
Drawing pin	drawing pin	ड्राइंग पिन
Envelope	lifaafaa	लिफाफा

Pile	gaddee	गंड़ी
Fountain pen	phaaunten pen	फाउन्टेन पेन
Glue	sares	सरेस
Gum	gond	गोंद
Ink	roshnaaee	रोश्नाई
Inkpot	dawaat	दवात
Invitation card	nimantran patra	निमंत्रण पत्र
Knife	chaaku	चाकू
Letter	patra	पत्र
Magazine	patrikaa	पत्रिका
Newspaper	akhbaar	अखबार
Nib	nib	निब
Paper	kaagaj	कागज
Paper-cutter	chaaku, chhuree	चाकू, छुरी
Paper-weight	kaagajdaab	कागजदाब
Pen	kalam	कलम
Pencil	pencil	पेंसिल
Pen-knife	kalam taraash	कलमतराश
Quill pen	par kee kalam	पर की कलम
Receipt book	raseed bahee	रसीद बही
Register	khaataa	खाता
Revenue stamp	raseedee tikat	रसीदी टिकट
Rubber	rabar	रबड़
Rubber stamp	rabar kee mohar	रबड़ की मोहर
Seal	muhar	मुहर
Sealing-wax	laakh	लाख
Scissors	kainchee	कैंची
Stamps	tikat	टिकट

Table	tebul	टेबुल
Tag	doree keeldaar	डोरी कीलदार
Visiting card	bhent kaard	भेंट कार्ड
Waste-paper	raddee kaagaj	रद्दी कागज
Waste-paper basket	raddee kaagaj	रद्दी कागज
	kee tokree	की टोकरी
Wire	taar	तार

VIII RELATIONSHIPS

Mother	maan, maataa	माँ, माता
Father	pitaa, baap	पिता, बाप
Brother	bhaaee	भाई
Sister	bahan	बहन
Husband	pati	पति
Wife	patnee	पत्नी
Son	betaa, putra	बेटा, पुत्र
Daughter	betee, putree	बेटी, पुत्री
Nephew (brother's son)	bhateejaa	भतीजा
Nephew (sister's son)	bhaanjaa	भांजा
Niece (brother's daughter)	bhateejee	भतीजी
Niece (sister's daughter)	bhaanjee	भांजी
Uncle (father's younger brother)	chaachaa, kaakaa	चाचा, काका
Aunt (father's younger brother's wife)	chaachee, kaakee	चाची, काकी
Uncle (mother's brother)	maamaa	मामा
Aunt (mother's brother's wife)	maamee	मामी

Brother-in-law (sister's husband)	bahnoee, jeejaa	बहनोई, जीजा
Brother-in-law (wife's brother)	saalaa	साला
Sister-in-law (wife's sister)	saalee	साली
Sister-in-law (elder brother's wife)	bhaabhee	भाभी
Aunt (father's sister)	phoofee, buvaa	फूफी, बुआ
Uncle (father's sister's husband)	phoopha	फूफा
Grandfather (paternal)	daadaa	दादा
Grandmother (paternal)	daadee	दादी
Grandfather (maternal)	naanaa	नाना
Grandmother (maternal)	naanee	नानी
Grandson (son's son)	potaa	पोता
Grand-daughter (son's daughter)	potee	पोती
Grandson (daughter's son)	natee	नाती
Granddaughter (daughter's daughter)	natin	नातिन
Grandchildren	natee pote	नाती पोते
Son-in-law	damad, jamaee	दामाद, जमाई
Dauther-in-law	bahu	बहू
Step mother	sautelee man	सौतेली माँ
Step father	sautela baap	सौतेना बाप
Step son	sautela beta	सौतेला बेटा

Step daughter	sautelee betee	सौतेली बेटी
Step brother	sautela bhaee	सौतेला भाई
Step sister	sautelee bahan	सौतेली बहन
Bridegroom	var	वर
Bride	vadhu	वधू
Co-wife	saut	सौत
Father-in-law (wife's father)	sasur	ससुर
Mother-in-law (wife's mother)	saas	सास
Uncle (father's elder brother)	tau	ताऊ
Aunt (father's elder brother's wife)	taee	ताई
Uncle (mother's sister's husband)	mausa	मौसा
Aunt (mother's sister)	mausee	मौसी
Brother-in-law (husband's sister's husband)	nandoee	ननदोई
Brother-in-law (husband's elder brother)	jeth	जेठ
Brother-in-law (husband's younger brother)	devar	देवर
Sister-in-law (husband's sister)	nanad	ननद
Sister-in-law (wife's brother's wife)	salhaj	सलहज
Son's wife's father	samdhee	समधी
Daughter's	samdhee	समधी

husband's father		
Son's wife's mother	samdhin	समधिन
Daughter's husband's mother	samdhin	समधिन
Woman	aurat, stree, naaree	औरत, स्त्री, नारी
Widow	vidhvaa	विधवा
Widower	vidhur	विधुर
Boy	larkaa	लड़का
Girl	larkee	लड़की
Man	aadmee	आदमी
Parents	maan baap	मां-बाप
Friend	dost, mitra	दोस्त, मित्र
Guest	mehmaan	मेहमान
Host	mezbaan	मेज़बान
Neighbour	parosee	पड़ोसी
Marriage	shaadee	शादी
Engagement	mangnee	मंगनी
Divorce	talaak	तलाक
Family	parivaar	परिवार
Relative	rishtedaar	रिश्तेदार
Relationship	rishtaa	रिश्ता
Wedding	shaadee	शादी

Chapter 5

Days, Months, Year, Numbers, Seasons, Directions, Colours & Greetings

I. DAYS

Afternoon	dopahar	दोपहर
Day	din	दिन
Day after yesterday	parsaun (beetaa huaa) din	परसों (बीता हुआ) दिन
Day after tomorrow	parsaun (aanewaalaa)	परसों (आने वाला)
Evening	shaam	शाम
Fortnight	pakhwaaraa	पखवाड़ा
Morning	subah	सुबह
Midnight	aadhee raat	आधीरात
Period	avadhi	अवधि
Time	samay	समय
Today	aaj	आज
Tomorrow	kal (anewaalaa)	कल (आने वाला)
Week	saptaah	सप्ताह
Yesterday	kal (beetaa huaa)	कल (बीता हुआ)
Monday	somvaar	सोमवार
Tuesday	mangalvaar	मंगलवार
Wednesday	budhvaar	बुधवार
Thursday	brihaspativaar	बृहस्पतिवार
Friday	shukravaar	शुक्रवार
Saturday	shanivaar	शनिवार
Sunday	ravivaar	रविवार
X'mas	baraadin	बड़ा दिन

II. MONTHS

Month	maheena, maas	महीना, मास
April	अप्रैल	chait	चैत
May	मई	baisaakh	बैसाख
June	जून	jaishta	ज्येष्ठ
July	जुलाई	ashaarh	आषाढ़
August	अगस्त	saawan	सावन
September	सितम्बर	bhaado	भादों
October	अक्टूबर	aashwin	अश्विन
November	नवम्बर	kaartik	कार्तिक
December	दिसम्बर	aghan	अगहन
January	जनवरी	poos, paush	पूस, पोष
February	फरवरी	maagh	माघ
March	मार्च	phaagun	फागुन

III. YEAR

Year	saal, varsh	साल, वर्ष
Decade	dashak	दशक
Century	sadee, shataabadi	सदी, शताब्दी

IV. NUMBERS

1	One	ek	एक
2	Two	do	दो
3	Three	teen	तीन
4	Four	chaar	चार
5	Five	paanch	पांच
6	Six	chhah	छः

7	Seven	saat	सात
8	Eight	aath	आठ
9	Nine	nau	नौ
10	Ten	das	दस
11	Eleven	gyaarah	ग्यारह
12	Twelve	baarah	बारह
13	Thirteen	terah	तेरह
14	Fourteen	chaudah	चौदह
15	Fifteen	pandrah	पन्द्रह
16	Sixteen	solah	सोलह
17	Seventeen	satrah	सतरह
18	Eighteen	athaarah	अठारह
19	Nineteen	unnees	उन्नीस
20	Twenty	bees	बीस
21	Twenty One	ekkees	इक्कीस
22	Twenty Two	baaees	बाईस
23	Twenty Three	teis	तेईस
24	Twenty Four	chaubees	चौबीस
25	Twenty Five	pachchees	पच्चीस
26	Twenty Six	chhabbees	छब्बीस
27	Twenty Seven	sattaaees	सत्ताईस
28	Twenty Eight	athaaees	अठाईस
29	Twenty Nine	unnatees	उनतीस
30	Thirty	tees	तीस
31	Thirty One	ekatees	इकतीस
32	Thirty Two	battees	बत्तीस
33	Thirty Three	tentees	तैंतीस
34	Thirty Four	chauntees	चौंतीस

35	Thrity Five	paintees	पैंतीस
36	Thirty Six	chhattees	छत्तीस
37	Thirty Seven	saintees	सैंतीस
38	Thirty Eight	artees	अड़तीस
39	Thirty Nine	unchaalees	उनचालीरु
40	Forty	chaalees	चालीस
41	Forty One	ektaalees	इकतालीस
42	Forty Two	byaalees	बयालीस
43	Forty Three	trtaalees	तितालीस
44	Forty Four	chauvaalees	चौवालीस
45	Forty Five	paintaalees	पैंतालीस
46	Forty Six	chhiyaalees	छियालीस
47	Forty Seven	saintalees	सैंतालीस
48	Forty Eight	artaalees	अड़तालीस
49	Forty Nine	unchaas	उनचास
50	Fifty	pachaas	पचास
51	Fifty One	ikaavan	इकावन
52	Fifty Two	baavan	बावन
53	Fifty Three	trepan	त्रेपन
54	Fifty Four	chauvan	चौवन
55	Fifty Five	pachpan	पचपन
56	Fifty Six	chhappan	छप्पन
57	Fifty Seven	sattaavan	सत्तावन
58	Fifty Eight	athaavan	अठावन
59	Fifty Nine	unsath	उनसठ
60	Sixty	saath	साठ
61	Sixty One	iksath	इकसठ
62	Sixty Two	baasath	बासठ

63	Sixty Three	tirsath	तिरसठ
64	Sixty Four	chaunsath	चौसठ
65	Sixty Five	painsath	पैंसठ
66	Sixty Six	chhiyasaath	छियासठ
67	Sixty Seven	sarsath	सरसठ
68	Sixty Eight	arsath	अड़सठ
69	Sixty Nine	unhattar	उनहत्तर
70	Seventy	sattar	सत्तर
71	Seventy One	ikhattar	इकहत्तर
72	Seventy Two	bahattar	बहत्तर
73	Seventy Three	tihattar	तिहत्तर
74	Seventy Four	chauhattar	चौहत्तर
75	Seventy Five	pachhattar	पचहत्तर
76	Seventy Six	chhihattar	छिहत्तर
77	Seventy Seven	sathattar	सतहत्तर
78	Seventy Eight	athhattar	अठहत्तर
79	Seventy Nine	unnasee	उन्नासी
80	Eighty	assee	अस्सी
81	Eighty One	ikaasee	इकासी
82	Eighty Two	bayaasee	बयासी
83	Eighty Three	tiraasee	तिरासी
84	Eighty Four	chauraasee	चौरासी
85	Eighty Five	pachaasee	पचासी
86	Eighty Six	chhiyaasee	छियासी
87	Eighty Seven	sattaasee	सत्तासी
88	Eighty Eight	athaasee	अठासी
89	Eighhty Nine	navaasee	नवासी
90	Ninety	nabbe	नब्बे

91	Ninety One	ikaanve	इकानवे
92	Ninety Two	baanve	बानवे
93	Ninety Three	tiraanve	तिरानवे
94	Ninety Four	chauraanve	चौरानवे
95	Ninety Five	panchaanve	पंचानवे
96	Ninety Six	chhiyaanve	छियानवे
97	Ninety Seven	sattaanve	सत्तानवे
98	Ninety Eight	athaanve	अठानवे
99	Ninety Nine	ninyaanve	निन्यानवे
100	Hundred	sau	सौ

V SEASONS

Autumn	sharad	शरद
Rains	barsaat	बरसात
Season	ritu	ऋतु
Summer	garmee	गरमी
Spring	basant	बसन्त
Winter	sardee	सरदी

VI DIRECTIONS

Direction	dishaa	दिशा
East	poorv	पूर्व
West	pashchim	पश्चिम
North	uttar	उत्तर
South	dakshin	दक्षिण

VII. COLOURS

Bright	chamkeelaa	चमकीला
Blue	neelaa	नीला
Black	kaalaa	काला
Brown	bhooraa	भूरा
Colour	rang	रंग
Gold	sunahraa	सुनहरा
Green	haraa	हरा
Olive	menhdee	मेंहदी
Pink/Rosy	gulaabee	गुलाबी
Purple	bainganee	बैंगनी
White	safhed	सफेद

VIII GREETINGS

Good morning	suprabhaat	सुप्रभात
Good noon	baraah baje	बारह बजे का
	kaa salaam	सलाम
Good day	din kaa salaam	दिन का सलाम
Good evening	shaam kaa salaam	शाम का सलाम
Good night	raat kee vidaaee	रात की बिदाई
Namaste	namaste	नमस्ते
Namaskar	namaskaar	नमस्कार
O.K.	sab theek	सब ठीक
See-off	vidaaee	विदाई
Thank you	dhanyavaad	धन्यवाद
Welcome	svaagatam	स्वागतम्

Chapter 6

Health & Ailments, Musical Instruments, Arts & Literature, Games & Sports, Trades & Professions

I HEALTH & AILMENTS

Acidity	amlpitt	अम्लपित्त
Acne	muhaasaà	मुँहासा
Ailments	rog, vyaadhiyaan	रोग, व्याधियां
Asthma	damaa	दमा
Baldness	ganjaapan	गंजापन
Belching	dakaar	डकार
Bile	pitt	पित्त
Blindness	andhaapan	अंधापन
Breath	saans	सांस
Bronchitis	kaas	कास
Cataract	motiyaabind	मोतियाबिंद
Chilblain	bivaee	बिबाई
Chill	thand	ठंड
Cholera	haijaa	हैजा
Conjunctivitis	aankha anaa	आंख आना
Constipation	kabjiyat	कब्जियत
Consumption	kshay	क्षय
Coryza	jukaam	जुकाम
Cough	khaansee	खांसी
Diabetes	bahumootra	बहुमूत्र
Diarrhoea	atisaar	अतिसार
Disease	rog	रोग

English	Transliteration	Hindi
Dumbness	goongaapan	गूंगापन
Dwarfness	baunaapan	बौनापन
Dysentry	pechish	पेचिश
Eczema	ukvat	उकवत
Epilepsy	mirgee	मिरगी
Fever	jwar	बुखार
Fistula	bhagandar	भगन्दर
Giddiness	chakkar	चक्कर
Gland	giltee	गिलटी
Gonorrhoea	sujak	सुजाक
Griping	maror	मरोड़
Health	swaasthya	स्वास्थ्य
Hernia	aant utarnaa	आंत उत
Hiccup	hichkee	हिचकँ
Hunger	bhookh	भूख
Hydrocele	andvriddhi	अंडवृद्धि
Indigestion	ajeern	अजीर्ण
Insomnia	neend na aanaa	नींद ना आना
Itches	khujli	खुजली
Jaundice	peelya	पीलिया
Leprosy	korh	कोढ़
Leucorrhoea	shwet kushth	श्वेत कुष्ठ
Leucorrhoea	swat	स्वेत
Madness	paagalpan	पागलपन
Mole	massa	मस्सा
Nausea	okaaee	ओकाई
Pain	dard	दर्द
Paralysis	lakvaa	लकवा

Phlegm	balgam	बलगम
Phlegm	kaph	कफ
Piles	bavaaseer	बवासीर
Pus	peeb	पीब
Rheumatism	gathiyaa	गठिया
Ringworm	daad	दाद
Saliva	laar	लार
Short-sightedness	alp-drishti	अल्प-दृष्टि
Sinus	naasur	नासूर
Sleep	neend	नींद
Sneezing	chheenk	छींक
Stone	pathree	पथरी
Stool	dast	दस्त
Sunstroke	loo lagnaa	लू लगना
Sweat	paseenaa	पसीना
Swelling	soojan	सूजन
Thirst	pyaas	प्यास
Tumour	gaanth	गांठ
Typhus	kaalaa jwar	काला ज्वर
Urine	mootra, peshaab	मूत्र, पेशाब
Voice	swar	स्वर
Vomiting	kai	कै, उल्टी
Wound	ghaav	घाव
Yawning	ubaasee	उबासी

II MUSICAL INSTRUMENTS

| Bagpipe | masak baajaa | मसक बाजा |
| Bell | ghantaa | घंटा |

Bugle	bigul	बिगुल
Clarion	turhee	तुरही
Clarionet	shahnaaee	शहनाई
Cymbal	jhaanjh	झांझ
Drum	dugdugee	डुगडुगी
Flute	baansuree	बांसुरी
Harp	chang	चंग
Harmonium	harmoniyam	हारमोनियम
Guitar	sitaar	सितार
Piano	piyaano	पियानो
Tambourine	daph	डफ
Tomtom	dholak	ढोलक
Violin	violin	वायलिन
Whistle	seetee	सीटी

III ARTS & LITERATURE

Actor	abhinetaa	अभिनेता
Artist	kalaakaar	कलाकार
Actress	abhinetree	अभिनेत्री
Art	kala	कला
Audience	darshak	दर्शक
Dance	naach, nritya	नाच, नृत्य
Dancer	nartak	नर्तक
Drama	naatak	नाटक
Essay	nibandh	निबंध
Essayist	nibandhkaar	निबंधकार
Folk tale	lok kathaa	लोक कथा
Literature	saahitya	साहित्य
Music	sangeet	संगीत

Musician	sangeetkaar	संगीतकार
Novel	upanyaas	उपन्यास
Novelist	upanyaaskaar	उपन्यासकार
Poet	kavi	कवि
Poetry	kavita	कविता
Song	geet, gaanaa	गीत, गाना
Story	kahaanee	कहानी
Story-writer	kahaaneekaar	कहानीकार
Writer	lekhak	लेखक

IV GAMES & SPORTS

Ball	gend	गेंद
Cricket	criket	क्रिकेट
Defeat	haar	हार
Football	phutbaul	फुटबाल
Game	khel	खेल
Goal	gol	गोल
Goal-keeper	golkee	गोलकी
Group	dal	दल
Hockey	haukee	हॉकी
Kabaddi	kabaddee	कबड्डी
Ludo	looddo	लूडो
Pingpong	pingpong	पिंगपोंग
Player	khilaaree	खिलाड़ी
Playground	khel kaa maidaan	खेल का मैदान
Snake & Ladder	saanp aur seerhee	साँप और सीढ़ी
Sports	khel	खेल
Sportsman	khilaaree	खिलाड़ी

Team	teem	टीम
Tennis	tenis	टेनिस
To score a goal	gol denaa	गोल देना
Victory	jeet	जीत
Volleyball	vauleebaul	वॉलीबाल

V TRADES & PROFESSIONS

Artist	kaareegar	कारीग
Bookseller	kitaab farosh	किताब फरोश
Braiser	thatheraa	ठठेरा
Betel-seller	tamolee	तमोली
Book-binder	jildsaaj	जिल्दसाज
Broker	dalaal	दलाल
Baker	naanbaee	नानबाई
Barrister	barristar	बैरिस्टर
Beggar	bhikhaaree	भिखारी
Butler	bhandaaree	भण्डारी
Boatman	mallaah	मल्लाह
Blacksmith	lohaar	लोहार
Barbar	hajjaam	हज्जाम
Butcher	kasaaee	कसाई
Coachman	kochvaan	कोचवान
Compositor	taaip bithaane vaalaa	टाईप बिठाने वाला
Carpenter	barhaee	बढ़ई
Carrier	maal dhone waalaa	माल ढोने वाला
Clerk	munshee	मुंशी
Cook	rasoeeaa	रसोइया
Carder	dhuniyaan	धुनियां
Confectioner	halvaaee	हलवाई

Doctor	daaktar	डाक्टर
Drummer	tabalchee	तबलची
Druggist	davaavikretaa	दवा विक्रेता
Dyer	rangrej	रंगरेज
Dentist	daant banaane waalaa	दांत बनाने वाला
Draper	bajaaj	बजाज
Engineer	abhiyantaa	अभियन्ता
Examiner	pareekshak	परीक्षक
Enameller	meenaakar	मीनाकार
Editor	sampaadak	संपादक
Farmer	kisaan	किसान
Fisherman	machhuvaaraa	मछुआरा
Greengrocer	kunjraa	कुंजड़ा
Grocer	modee	मोदी
Glazier	sheeshaa lagaane waalaa	शीशा लगाने वाला
Groom	saees	साईस
Gardener	maalee	माली
Goldsmith	sunaar	सुनार
Hawker	phereewaalaa	फेरी वाला
Inspector	nireekshak	निरीक्षक
Jeweller	jauharee	जौहरी
Loader	laadnevaalaa	लादने वाला
Midwife	daaee	दाई
Milkman	aheer	दुधिया
Mason	raajmistree	राजमिस्त्री
Milkman	doodh vaalaa	दूधवाला
Manager	prabandhkarttaa	प्रबंध कर्ता

Messenger	doot	दूत
Merchant	saudaagar	सौदागर
Nurse	dhay	धाय
Oilman	telee	तेली
Perfumer	gandhee	गन्धी
Profession	peshaa	पेशा
Postman	daakiyaa	डाकिया
Photographer	photo utaarne waalaa	फोटो उतारने वाला
Proprietor	maalik	मालिक
Pleader	vakeel	वकील
Publisher	prakaashak	प्रकाशक
Parcher	bhoonjaa	भूंजा
Printer	mudrak	मुद्रक
Painter	rangsaaj	रंगसाज
Physician	vaidya	वैद्य
Retailer	khudraa vyaapaari	खुदरा व्यापारी
Repairer	marammat karne waalaa	मरम्मत करने वाला
Surgeon	jarraah	जर्राह
Sorcerer	jaadugar	जादूगर
Sailor	maanjhee	मांझी
Shoemaker	mochee	मोची
Shopkeeper	dukaandaar	दुकानदार
Sculptor	sangtaraash	संगतराश
Seedman	beej vikretaa	बीज विक्रेता
Trade	vyavasaay	व्यवसाय
Teacher	adhyaapak	अध्यापक
Turner	kharaadnewaalaa	खरादनेवाला

Typist	taaip karne	टाईप करने
	vaalaa	वाला
Treasury	khajaanchee	खजांची
Tailor	darjee	दर्जी
Vaccinator	tika laganawala	टीका लगनेवाला
Weaver	julaahaa	जुलाहा
Washerman	dhobee	धोबी
Waterman	kahaar	कहार
Watchman	pahredaar	पहरेदार
Washerwoman	dhobin	धोबिन
Clerk	lipik	लिपिक

Chapter 7
Around Town, States & Country, Politics & Government, High Officials

I. AROUND TOWN

Airport	hawaaee addaa	०वाई अड्डा
Bus	bas	बस
Bicycle	baay siekil	बाईसकिल
Bus-stand	bas-staind	बस स्टेन्ड
Building	imaarat	ईमारत
Bazar	baazaar	बाजार
Cart	bailgaaree	बैलगाड़ी
College	kaalej	कॉलेज
Court	kachaharee	कचहरी
Church	girjaaghar	गिरजाघर
Crowd	bheer	भीड़

Crossing	chauraahaa	चौराहा
Cinema	sinemaa	सिनेमा
Circus	sarkas	सर्कस
Ditch	khaaee	खाई
Drama	naatak	नाटक
Electricity	bijlee	बिजली
Electric pole	bijlee kaa khambhaa	बिजली का खम्भा
Fence	baaraa	बाड़ा
Field	khet	खेत
Farm	phaarm	फार्म
Gutter	naalaa	नाला
Gurudwara	gurudwaara	गुरुद्वारा
Ground	maidaan	मैदान
Hotel	hotal	होटल
Hut	jhonparee	झोंपड़ी
Hospital	aspataal	अस्पताल
Inn	saraay	सराय
Library	pustakaalay	पुस्तकालय
Lane	galee	गली
Mosque	masjid	मस्जिद
Motor cycle	motar saaeekil	मोटर साइकिल
Poster	postar	पोस्टर
Post Office	daakghar	डाकघर
Park	park	पार्क
Plants	paudhe	पौधे
Restaurant	restorant	रेस्टोरेन्ट
Rickshaw	rikshaa	रिक्शा
Road	sarak	सड़क

Sports	khelkood	खेलकूद
Scooter	skootar	स्कूटर
Station	steshan	स्टेशन
School	skool	स्कूल
Shop	dukaan	दुकान
Stadium	stadiaum	स्टेडियम
Tonga	taangaa	तांगा
Taxi	taksee	टैक्सी
Train	tren	ट्रैन
Tram	traam	ट्राम
Truck	truck	ट्रक
Three-wheeler	three-wheelar	थ्री-व्हीलर
Telegraph office	taarghar	तारघर
Temple	mandir	मन्दिर
Telephone	telephon	टेलीफोन
Tree	per	पेड़
Theatre	thiyetar	थियेटर
Wire	taar	तार
Zoo	chiriyaaghar	चिड़ियाघर

II AROUND COUNTRY & STATES

Christian	eesaaee	ईसाई
Country	desh	देश
Empire	saamraajya	साम्राज्य
Of Bihar	bihaaree	बिहारी
Of Assam	aasaamee	आसामी
Of Maharashtra	marathe	मराठी
Of Rajasthan	raajasthaanee	राजस्थानी
Of Nepal	nepaalee	नेपाली

Of Punjab	panjaabee	पंजाबी
Of Bengal	bangaalee	बंगाली
Of Madras	madraasee	मद्रासी
Of Marwar	maarwaaree	मारवाड़ी
Of Gujarat	gujraatee	गुजराती
Of Gorakhpur	gorakhpuri	गोरखपुरी
Of Sind	sindhee	सिंधी
Kingdom	riyaasat	रियासत
Motherland	maatribhoomi	मातृभूमि
Muslims	musalmaan	मुसलमान
Priest	purohit	पुरोहित
Province	pradesh	प्रदेश
State	raajya	राज्य

III POLITICS & GOVERNMENT

Administration	prashaasan	प्रशासन
Ambassador	raajdoot	राजदूत
Administrator	prashaasak	प्रशासक
Ballot paper	mat patra	मत पत्र
Ballot box	mat petee	मत पेटी
Court	kachaharee	कचहरी
Diplomat	raajnaayak	राजनायक
Democracy	loktantra	लोकतन्त्र
Election	chunaav	चुनाव
Embassy	raajdootaavaas	राजदूतावास
Federation	sangh	संघ
Federal	sangheeya	संघीय
Franchise	mataadhikaar	मताधिकार
Government	sarkar	सरकार

Independence	swatantrataa	स्वतन्त्रता
Imprisonment	kaid	कैद
Independence day	swaadheentaa divas	स्वाधीनता दिवस
Justice	nyaaya	न्याय
Judgment	faisalaa	फैसला
Judge	nyaayaadheesh	न्यायाधीश
Jail	karagar	कारागार
Law	kaanun	कानून
Lawyer	vakeel	वकील
Magistrate	maigistret	मजिस्ट्रेट
Municipality	nagarpaalika	नगरपालिका
National flag	raashtreeya jhandaa	राष्ट्रीय झंडा
Politics	raajneeti	राजनीति
Parliament	sansad	संसद
Parliament House	sansad bhavan	संसद भवन
Parliament member	sansad sadasya	संसद सदस्य
Republic day	gantantra divas	गणतन्त्र दिवस
Suit	mukadmaa	मुकदमा
Vote	mat	मत

IV HIGH OFFICIALS

President	rashtrapati	राष्ट्रपति
Vice President	upraashtrapati	उपराष्ट्रपति
Prime Minister	pradhaanmantree	प्रधानमंत्री
Chief Minister	mukhyamantree	मुख्यमंत्री
Cabinet Minister	kendreeya mantree	केन्द्रीय मंत्री
State Minister	raajyamantree	राज्यमंत्री
Deputy Minister	upmantree	उपमंत्री
Governor	raajyapaal	राज्यपाल

High Commissioner	haaee kamishnar	हाई कमिश्नर
Chief Justice	mukhya nyaayaadheesh	मुख्य न्यायाधीश
Secretary	sachiv	सचिव
President's House	raashtrapati bhawan	राष्ट्रपति भवन
Supreme Court	sarvochch nyaayaalaya	सर्वोच्च न्यायालय
Cabinet	mantrimandal	मंत्रिमण्डल
Army	senaa	सेना
Navy	nausenaa	नौ सेना
Air force	vayu senaa	वायु सेना

Chapter 8

Earth Nature, Planets, Trees, Stones, Metals & Minerals

I EARTH NATURE

Earth	Dharti/Jameen	धरती/जमीन
swarg	Heaven	स्वर्ग
hawa	Air	हवा
din	Day	दिन
subah	Morning	सुबह
aag	Fire	आग
nadee	River	नदी
Sky	aasman	आसमान
Hell	narak	नरक
Cloud	badal	बादल
Night	raat	रात

English	Transliteration	Hindi
Evening	shaam	शाम
Water	paanee	पानी
Stream	chashma	चश्मा
Lake	Jheel	झील
Sea	samudra	समुद्र
Forest	jangal	जंगल
Fog	kuhara	कुहरा
Hail	ole	ओले
Rain	varsha	वर्षा
Storm	toophaan	तूफान
Thunder	vojra	वज्र
Sunshine	dhoop	धूप
Weather	mausam	मौसम
Sun	sooraj	सूरज
Stars	taare	तारे
World	duniyaa	दुनिया
Ocean	mahaasaagar	महासागर
Mountain	parvat	पर्वत
Frost	paalaa	पाला
Ice	barph	बर्फ
Gale	aandhee	आंधी
Lightning	bijlee	बिजली
Shore	tat	तट
Shade	chhaayaa	छाया
Season	ritu	ऋतु
Moon	chaand	चांद
Milky way	aakaash gangaa	आकाश गंगा

II PLANETS

Venus	shukra	शुक्र
Saturn	shani	शनि
Mars	mangal	मंगल
Planet	graha	ग्रह
Sun	soorya	सूर्य
Mercury	budh	बुध
Jupiter	brihaspati	वृहस्पति

III TREE & ITS PARTS

Tree	per/vriksh	पेड़/वृक्ष
Mango	aam	आम
Pine	cheer	चीड़
Guava	amrood	अमरूद
Conifer	jhaaoo	झाऊ
Acacia	babool	बबूल
Bamboo	baans	बांस
Mahogany	mahoganee	महोगनी
Teak	saagwaan	सागवान
Cactus	senhur	सेंहुड़
Graft	kalam	कलम
Bud	kalee	कली
Thorn	kaantaa	कांटा
Stone	guthlee	गुठली
Pulp	goodaa	गूदा
Bark	chhal	छाल
Rind	chhilkaa	छिलका
Root	jar	जड़

Branch	tahnee	टहनी
Stem	dhar	धड़
Fibre	reshaa	रेशा
Seed	beej	बीज
Leaf	pattee	पत्ती
Juice	ras	रस
Wood	kaath	काठ

IV STONES, METALS & MINERALS

Mica	abhrak	अभ्रक
Touchstone	kasautee	कसौटी
Emery	kuroon	कुरून
Coal	koyla	कोयला
	(patthar kaa)	(पत्थर का)
Charcoal	koylaa	कोयला
	(lakree kaa)	(लकड़ी का)
Sulhur	gandhak	गंधक
Flint	chakmak	चकमक पत्थर
	patthar	
Zinc	jastaa	जस्ता
Steel	lohaa (pakkaa)	लोहा (पक्का)
Mercury	paaraa	पारा
Tin	raangaa	रांगा
Arsenic	sankhiyaa	संखिया
White lead	safedaa	सफेदा
Lead	seesaa	सीसा
Metal	dhaatu	धातु
Rock	chattaan	चट्टान
Bronze	kaskut	कसकुट

Bell-metal	kaansaa	कांसा
Chalk	khariyaa	खड़िया
Ochre	geroo	गेरू
Silver	chaandee	चांदी
Copper	taambaa	तांबा
Iron	lohaa	लोहा
Brass	peetal	पीतल
Bitumin	shilaajeet	शिलाजीत
Marble	sangamarmar	संगमरमर
Cinnabar	singaraph	सिंगरफ
Stone	patthar	पत्थर
Mineral	khanij	खनिज

Part-3

Social Phraseology, Administrative Terms, Foreign Words, Telegraphic Greetings, Short Letters, Popular Proverbs.

I. SOCIAL PHRASEOLOGY

Abductor	Apahartaa	अपहर्त्ता
Abide by	Paalan karnaa	पालन करना
Abridged edition	Sankshipta Sanskaran	संक्षिप्त संस्करण
Absconder	Bhagoraa	भगोड़ा
Accede to	Sweekaar karna	स्वीकार करना
Adult education	praurh shikshaa	प्रौढ़ शिक्षा
Adverting to	par dhyaan na dete hue	पर ध्यान न देते हुए
Agrarian reform	krishi sudhaar	कृषि सुधार

All out effort	bharsak prayatna	भरसक प्रयत्ल
All rights reserved	sarvaadhikaar surakshit	सर्वाधिकार सुरक्षित
As aforesaid	poorva kathnaanusaar	पूर्व कथनानुसार
As a general rule	saamaanyatah	सामान्यतः
As a matter of course	swabhaavatah	स्वभावतः
As a matter of fact	yathaartah	यथार्थतः
As a matter of right	saadhikaar	साधिकार
As a rule	niyamatah	नियमतः
As a whole	poornatah	पूर्णतः
As far as	jahaan tak	जहां तक
As far as practicable	jahaan tak vyavhaarya ho	जहां तक व्यवहार्य हो
As laid down	yathaanirdhaarit	यथानिर्धारित
As per detail	byore ke anusaar	ब्योरे के अनुसार
As proposed	yathaa prastaavit	यथाप्रस्तावित
As required	yathaa apekshit	यथाअपेक्षित
Backbiting	chugalkhoree	चुगलखोरी
Backbone	aadhaarstambha	आधारस्तम्भ
Background	prishta bhoomi	पृष्ठभूमि
Bad-blood	katutaa	कटुता
Bad debt	ashodhy rin	अशोध्य ऋण
Banquet hall	bhoj bhavan	भोज भवन
Bag and baggage	boriyaa bistar	बोरिया-बिस्तर

Beat about the bush	idhar udhar	इधर उधर की
	ki baten karnaa	बातें करना
Beat of drum	dhindhoraa	ढिंढोरा
Birth control	santati nigrah	संतति निग्रह
Birth-rate	janmaanupaat	जन्मानुपात
Birth-right	janmasiddh	जन्मसिद्ध
	adhikaar	अधिकार
Black-leg	juwaree,	जुआरी,
	hartalbhedee	हड़तालभेदी
Blood pressure	raktachaap	रक्तचाप
Bring home to	hridayangam karna	हृदयंगम करना
Bring to notice	dhyaan mein laanaa	ध्यान में लाना
Burial ground	kabristaan	कब्रिस्तान
Burning ground	shmashaan bhoomi	श्मशान भूमि
By-pass	up-maarga	उप-मार्ग
By products	upotpaad	उपोत्पाद
Civil right	naagrik adhikaar	नागरिक अधिकार
Civil marriage	panjee vivaaha	पंजी विवाह
Civil matter	naagrik vishay	नागरिक विषय
Code-word	sanket shabd	संकेत शब्द
Co-heir	sahottaraadhikaaree	सहोत्तराधिकारी
Come of age	baalig	बालिग
Composite culture	saamaasik sanskriti	सामासिक संस्कृति
Condolence	samvednaa	संवेदना संदेश
message	sandesh	
Conjugal rights	daampatya adhikaar	दाम्पत्य अधिकार
Cow-in-calf	gaabhin gaay	गाभिन गाय
Cow-in-milk	dudhaaru gaay	दुधारू गाय

Dairy-farm	dugdhashaalaa	दुग्धशाला
Dark-room	tamomay koshth	तमोमय कोष्ठ
Day-to-day	din pratidin	दिन प्रतिदिन
Dead-letter	nirgat patra	निर्गत पत्र
Deadlock	gati avarodh	गति अवरोध
Dead-stock	binaa bikaa huaa maal	बिना बिका हुआ माल
Denovo	naye sire se	नये सिरे से
Dissolute	durvyasanee, lampat	दुर्व्यसनी, लापट
Ditto	tathaiv, tadaiva	तथैव, तदैव
Eavesdropper	aar men chip kar sunnewaalaa	आड़ में छिपकर सुननेवाला
Elopement	sah palaayan	सह पलायन
En block	ek saath	एक साथ
En route	maarg men, jaate hue	मार्ग में, जाते हुए
Extrovert	bahirmukh	बहिर्मुख
Eye-sight	drishti shakti	दृष्टि शक्ति
Face value	ankit moolya	अंकित मूल्य
Fair sex	ramnee varg, stree jaati	रमणी वर्ग, स्त्री जाति
Flat rate	ek bhaav	एक भाव
Floating bridge	tairnewaalaa pul	तैरने वाला पुल
Folk-song	lok-geet	लोक-गीत
Full brother	sagaa bhaaee	सगा भाई
God-daughter	dharm putree	धर्म पुत्री
Godfather	dharm-pitaa	धर्म-पिता

Godmother	dharm-maataa	धर्म-माता
Good faith	sadbhaav	सद्भाव
Goods train	maalgaaree	मालगाड़ी
Gross negligence	bhaaree laaparwaahee	भारी लापरवाही
Half-blood	sautelaa khoon	सौतेला खून
Half-brother	sautelaa bhaaee	सौतेला भाई
Highway	raajmaarg	राजमार्ग
Housekeeper	grihpaal	गृहपाल
Hunger-strike	bhookh hartaal	भूख हड़ताल
Imbroglio	uljhan, jatiltaa	उलझन, जटिलता
Incognito	gupt roop se	गुप्त रूप से
In good faith	sadbhaavnaa se	सद्भावना से
In good health	swastha	स्वस्थ
In good order	suvyavasthit	सुव्यवस्थित
In infinitum	anant tak	अनन्त तक
In lieu of	ke badle	के बदले
In loco	uchit sthaan men	उचित स्थान में
In toto	poorntayaa	पूर्णतया
Juvenile delinquency	baal apraadh	बाल अपराध
Kindergarden	shishu vihar	शिशु विहार
Land mark	pramukh sthan	प्रमुख स्थान
Libel	apmaanlekh, nindaalekh	अपमान लेख, निन्दालेख
Maiden speech	pratham vyaakhyaan	प्रथम व्याख्यान
Malpractice	dushkarm, duraachaar	दुष्कर्म, दुराचार

Man of blood	lauh purush	लौह पुरुष
Marriage dissolution	vivaah bhang	विवाह भंग
Marriage, Nullity of	vivaah raddkaran	विवाह रद्दकरण
Maternity centre	prasooti kendra	प्रसूति केंद्र
Midwifery	daaeegiree	दाईगिरी
Moral turpitude	anaitik aachaar, naitik patan	अनैतिक आचार, नैतिक पतन
Natural child	anauras santan	अनौरस संतान
Nomeneclature	shabdaavalee, naamaavalee	शब्दावली, नामावली
Nonsense	arthheen, nirarthak	अर्थहीन, निरर्थक
Oblivion	vismriti	विस्मृति
Obliquy	nindokti	निन्दोक्ति
Obnoxious	ghrinit, kutsit	घृणित, कुत्सित
Obscene	ashleel	अश्लील
Obsolete	aprachalit	अप्रचलित
Overture	prastaav	प्रस्ताव
Overturn	ulat denaa, palatnaa	उलट देना, पलटना
Pendown strike	lekhneeband hartal	लेखनीबंद हड़ताल
Poet laureate	rajkavi	राजकवि
Polluted water	dooshit jal	दूषित जल
Posthumous	marnottar	मरणोत्तर
Post-nupital	vivaahotar	विवाहोत्तर
Raise an alarm	hallaa machaanaa	हल्ला मचाना
Ring-leader	toli kaa mukhiyaa	टोली का मुखिया
Round worms	kechuvaa	केचुआ
Rural dispensary	graam aushdhaalay	ग्राम औषधालय

Sex perversity	apraakritik kaam vaasnaa	अप्राकृतिक काम वासना
Sister tutor	upchaar shikshikaa	उपचार शिक्षिका
Staff-room	adhyaapak kakshaa	अध्यापक कक्ष
Sunstroke	loo, loo lagnaa	लू, लू लगना
Topsy-turvy	ulat-pulat	उलट-पुलट
Top to toe	nakh shikhaant	नख शिखान्त
Tution fee	shikshan shulka	शिक्षण शुल्क
Unskilled	apraveen	अप्रवीण
Untenable	atikaau	अटिकाऊ
Upkeep	dekhrekh	देखरेख
Vis-a-vis	aamne saamne	आमने सामने
Viva-voce	maukhik	मौखिक
Vulgar	ashisht, ashleel	अशिष्ट, अश्लील
Vulnerable	maarmik	मार्मिक
Weaker sex	ablaa, stree	अबला, स्त्री
Well-being	kalyaan	कल्याण
Well-to-do	sampanna	सम्पन्न
Yours faithfully	bhavannishth	भवन्निष्ठ
Yours sincerely	bhavadeeya	भवदीय

II ADMINISTRATIVE TERMS

A

Abdication of throne	sinhaasan-tyaag	सिंहासन-त्याग
Accession of a state	raajya kaa sahmilan	राज्य का सहमिलन

Account Book	lekhaa pustak	लेखापुस्तक
Accountant General	mahaalekhapaal	महालेखपाल
Additional judge	atirikt nyaayaa-dheesh	अतिरिक्त न्यायाधीश
Ad Hoc Committee	etadarth samiti	एतदर्थ समिति
Adjutant-General	mahaasahaayak	महासहायक
Administer oath	shapath dilaanaa	शपथ दिलाना
Administration	prashaasan	प्रशासन
Administrative	prashaasakeeya	प्रशासकीय
Adult Franchise	praurh mataadhikaar	प्रौढ़ मताधिकार
Advisory Council	mantranaa parishad	मंत्रणा-परिषद
Advocate General	mahaadhivaktaa	महाधिवक्ता
A idavit	halaphnaamaa	हलफनामा
Amoassador	raajdoot	राजदूत
Ambulatory Court	chal nyaayaalay	चल न्यायालय
Amendment Act	sanshodhak vidhaan	संशोधक विधान
Anti-corruption	bhrashtaachaar-virodhee	भ्रष्टाचार-विरोधी
Appellate Court	appeel nyaayaalay	अपील न्यायालय
Appointing Authority	niyukti adhikaaree	नियुक्ति अधिकारी
Armament	shastrasajjit sainya	शस्त्रसज्जित सैन्य
Armoury	shastraagaar	शस्त्रागार
Assembly, Legislative	vidhaan sabhaa	विधानसभा
Assembly, Constituent	samvidhaan sabhaa	संविधान सभा
Audit	hisaab kee jaanch	हिसाब की जांच
Audit Officer	lekhaa pareekshak	लेखा परीक्षक
Auditor-General	mahaalekhaa pareekshak	महालेखा-परीक्षक

B

Ballot	matpatra, guptmat	मतपत्र, गुप्तमत
Battalion	paidal senaa kee tukree	पैदल सेना की टुकड़ी
Bilingual state	dwibhaashee raajya	द्विभाषी राज्य
Breach of Peace	shaantibhang	शांतिभंग
Breache of Law	vidhi-bhang	विधि-भंग
Bureaucracy	naukarshaahee	नौकरशाही
By-election	up-nirvaachan	उप-निर्वाचन

C

Cabinet	mantrimandal	मंत्रिमंडल
Cantonment	chhaawnee	छावनी
Canvass	mat yaachnaa/ prachaar karnaa	मत याचना/ प्रचार करना
Cease-fire	yuddh viraam	युद्धविराम
Census	jan-garnaa	जन-गणना
Central	kendreeya	केन्द्रीय
Centralization	keandreeyakaran	केन्द्रीयकरण
Chancellor	kulpati	कुलपति
Charter	raajlekh, sanad	राजलेख, सनद
Chief Minister	mukhyamantree	मुख्यमंत्री
Chief Justice	mukhya nyaa-yaadhipati	मुख्य नयायाधिपति
C.I.D.	khuphiyaa pulis	खुफिया पुलिस
Circle Inspector	halkaa inspektar	हलका इन्सपेक्टर
Circuit House	golghar, laat saahab kee kothee	गोलघर, लाट साहब की कोठी
Civil Court	deewaanee kachharee	दीवानी कचहरी

Civil defence	pratirakshaa	प्रतिरक्षा
Civil procedure	vyavaahaar vidhi	व्यवहार विधि
Code	sanhitaa	संहिता
Civil war	grihayuddh	गृहयुद्ध
Coalition Government	sanyukt shaasan	संयुक्त शासन
Collateral security	sahvartee pratibhooti	सहवर्ती प्रतिभूति
Colonization	upniveshan	उपनिवेशन
Commission	aayog	आयोग
Commissioner	aayukt	आयुक्त
Comptroller	lekhaa-niyantrak	लेखा-नियंत्रक
Condominium	dwiraajya	द्विराज्य
Constitution	samvidhaan	संविधान
Co-operative	sahkaaree	सहकारी
Council of States	raajya parishad	राज्य परिषद
Council Session	parishad kaa adhiveshan	परिषद का अधिवेशन
Court of Small Causes	laghu nyaayaalay	लघुवाद न्यायालय
Crime-police	apraadhshodhan pulis	अपराधशोधन पुलिस
Criminal Court	dand nyaayaalay	दण्ड न्यायालय
Crown Counsel	sarkaaree vakeel	सरकारी वकील
Custodian	sanrakshak	संरक्षक
Custom Officer	bahishulk adhikaaree	बहिःशुल्क अधिकारी

D

English	Transliteration	Hindi
Dangerous	haanikaarak aushadi	हानिकारक औषधि
Drugs Act	adhiniyam	अधिनियम
Dealing clerk	etatsambandhee lipik	एतत्संबंधी लिपिक
Decentralization	vikendreekaran	विकेन्द्रीयकरण
committee	samiti	समिति
Decreeholder	nyayapatra-graahee	न्यायपत्रग्राही
Decree-nisi	sapratibandh nyaayapatra	सप्रतिबन्ध न्यायपत्र
Defence Department	surakshaa vibhaag	सुरक्षा विभाग
De jure ruler	vidhaanaanukul shaasak	विधानानुकूल शासक
Delegation	shishtmandal	शिष्टमंडल
Democracy	gantantra, loktantra	गणतंत्र, लोकतंत्र
Depressed classes	dalit jaatiyaan	दलित जातियां
Deputy Chairman	up-sabhaapati	उप-सभापति
Deputy Secretary	up-sachiv	उप-सचिव
Detention order	nirodhaadesh	निरोधादेश
Development Board	vikaas parishad	विकास परिषद
Co-ordination	vikaas sahyog	विकास सहयोग
Dictator	taanaashaah	तानाशाह
D.I.G. Police	mahaa-dheekshak	महाअधीक्षक
Directorate	nideshaalay	निदेशालय
Director of Education	shikshaa nideshak	शिक्षा निदेशक
Disarmament	nihshastree-karan	निःशस्त्रीकरण
District Board	janpad parishad	जनपद परिषद
District Magistrate	janpadaadheesh	जनपदाधीश

| District Municipal Board | janpad nagarpaalikaa | जनपद नगरपालिका |
| Division Bench | khand nyayapeeth | खण्ड न्यायपीठ |

E

Editor	sampaadak	संपादक
Editor Managing	prabandh sampaadak	प्रबंध संपादक
Educational Code	shikshaa vidhi sanhitaa	शिक्षा विधि संहिता
Education Department	shikshaa vibhaag	शिक्षा विभाग
Election petition	chunaav yaachikaa	चुनाव याचिका
Election Tribunal	nirvaachan adhikaran	निर्वाचन अधिकरण
Electoral constituency	nirvaachan kshetra	निर्वाचन क्षेत्र
Electrical installation	vidyut pratishthan	विधुत प्रतिष्ठान
Embezzlement	gaban	गबन
Emissary	guptadoot	गुप्तदूत
Employment	sevaa-yojan	सेवा-योजन
Exchange	kaaryaalay	कार्यालय
En camerao trial	guptkaksh vichaar	गुप्तकक्ष विचार
Establishment charges	sthaapanaa prahbhaar	स्थापना प्रभार
Excellency, His	mahaamaanya, Mahaamahim	महामान्य, महामहिम
Excise duty	utpaadan shulk	उत्पादन शुल्क
Excise Minister	aabkaree mantree	आबकारी मंत्री
Executive	kaaryakaarinee	कार्यकारिणी

Authority	sattaadhikaaree	सत्ताधिकारी
Ex-officio	paden, pad ke naate	पदेन, पद के नाते
Ex-parte	ek paksheeya	एकपक्षीय
Ex-patriate	desh se nikaal dena	देश से निकाल देना
Explanatory	vyaakhyatamak	व्याख्यात्मक
memorandum	smritipatra	स्मृतिपत्र
Export tax	niryaat kar	निर्यात कर
Extension of post	padkaal-vriddhi	पदकाल-वृद्धि
External affairs	vaideshik kaarya	वैदेशिक कार्य
Extra-judicial	nyaayaatirikt	न्यायातिरिक्त

F

Faculty Law	vidhi-shaakhaa	विधि-शाखा
Famine project	durbhiksh-yojanaa	दुर्भिक्ष-योजना
Favoured nation	anugraheet raashtra	अनुग्रहीत राष्ट्र
Federal Court	sangh nyaayaalay	संघ न्यायालय
Federation	raj-sangh	राज-संघ
Finance Committee	artha-samiti	अर्थ-समिति
Financial stability	vitteeya sthaayitva	वितीय स्थायित्व
Fire brigade	agni-shamak dal/yantra	अग्निशामक दल/यंत्र
First-aid	prathmo-pachaar	प्रथमोपचार
F.I.R.	praarambhik soochanaa	प्रारंभिक सूचना
Fishery development	meenkshetra vikaas	मीनक्षेत्र विकास
Flag-staff	pataaka dandaa	पताका डंडा
Food-Controller	khaadya niyantrak	खाद्य नियंत्रक
Foreign currencies	videshee mudraaen	विदेशी मुद्राएं
Forest Ranger	vankshetrapal	वन-क्षेत्रपाल

Formal Education	yathaavidhi shikshaa	यथाविधि शिक्षा
Franchise	mataadhikaar	मताधिकार
Full bench	poorna nyaayapeeth/ nyaayaadheesh varga	पूर्ण न्यायपीठ/ न्यायाधीश वर्ग
Functus officio	samaaptaa-dhikaar	समाप्ताधिकार

G

Gazetted Service	raajpatrit sevaa	राजपत्रित सेवा
General Administration Deptt.	saamaanya prashaasan vibhaag	सामान्य प्रशासन विभाग
General Election	aam chunaav	आम चुनाव
General Manager	mahaa-prabandhak	महाप्रबंधक
G.O.I.	bhaarat sarkaar	भारत सरकार
G.O.	sarkaree aagyaa	सरकारी आज्ञा
Governing Body	prabandh mandal	प्रबंध मंडल
Government affairs	raajkaaj, sarkaaree kaam	राजकाज, सरकारी काम
Government House	raajbhawan	राजभवन
Governor	raajyapaal	राज्यपाल
Guard of honour	sainik abhivaadan	सैनिक अभिवादन

H

Habeas corpus	vaiyaktik swatantrataa niyam	वैयक्तिक स्वतंत्रता नियम
Headquarters	mukhyaalay	मुख्यालय
Her Excellency	mahaamaanya	महामान्या

High Commissioner for India	bhaarat ke uchch aayukta	भारत के उच्च आयुक्त
High Power Committee	uch shakti samiti	उच्च शक्ति समिति
Hoisting of flag	dhwajaarohan, jhandottolan	ध्वजारोहण, झंडोत्तोलन
Home Department (criminal)	griha vibhaag (faujdaaree)	गृह विभाग (फौजदारी)
Home Department (Jails)	griha vibhaag (kaaraagaar)	गृह विभाग (कारागार)
Home Department (Police)	griha vibhaag (pulis)	गृह विभाग (पुलिस)
Hon'ble Minister	maanneeya mantree	माननीय मंत्री
Horticulture	udyaan shaastra	उद्यान-शास्त्र
Hydro-electric	jal-bijlee	जल-बिजली

I

I.A.S.	bharateeya prashaasan sevaa	भारतीय प्रशासन सेवा
Imperialism	saamraajyavaad	साम्राज्यवाद
Imperial Service	raashtreeya sevaa	राष्ट्रीय सेवा
Independence Day	swatantrataa divas	स्वतंत्रता दिवस
Indian Air Force	bhaarteeya vaayu senaa	भारतीय वायु सेना
Indian Arms Act	bhaarteeyaa shastra vidhaan	भारतीय शस्त्र विधान
Indian languages	bhaarteeya lokbhaahaa	भारतीय लोकभाषा-
Deptt.	prasaar vibhaag	प्रसार विभाग
Industries Deptt.	udyog vibhaag	उद्योग विभाग

Information Deptt.	soochna vibhaag	सूचना विभाग
Insolvent states	divaaliyaa riyaasaten	दिवालिया रियासतें
Inspector General	mahaa nireekshak	महानिरीक्षक
Intelligence Bureau	guptavaartaa vibhaag	गुप्तवार्ता विभाग
Internal security	aanterik surakshaa	आन्तरिक सुरक्षा
Intra-State	raajyaabhyantar	राज्याभ्यन्तर

J

Jail, Central	kendreeya kaaraagriha	केन्द्रीय कारागृह
Jail, District	janpad kaaraagriha	जनपद कारागृह
Joint Secretary	sanyukt sachiv	संयुक्त सचिव
Judicial Authority	nyaayik praadhikaaree	न्यायिक प्राधिकारी
Juvenile Court	baal nyaayaalay	बाल न्यायालय

L

Laboratory attendant	prayogashaala parichar	प्रयोग शाला परिचर
Labour dispute	shramik vivaad	श्रमिक विवाद
Labour union	shramik sangh	श्रमिक संघ
Land Acquisition Officer	bhooarjan adhikaaree	भूअर्जन अधिकारी
Law and order	shaanti aur vyavasthaa	शांति और व्यवस्था
Leader of the House	sadan kaa netaa	सदन का नेता
Legal advisor	vidhik paraa-marshdaataa	विधिक परामर्शदाता
Legislative procedure	vidhaayee prakriyaa	विधायी प्रक्रिया
Letter of adminis-tration	prabandhaadhi-kaar patra	प्रबन्धाधिकार पत्र

Letter of attorney	abhikartaa patra	अभिकर्ता पत्र
Local Government	sthaaneeya sarkaar	स्थानीय सरकार
Local Self Government	sthaaneeya swaraajya	स्थानीय स्वराज्य
L.D.A.	nimnavarga sahaayak	निम्नवर्ग सहायक
L.D.C.	nimnavarga lipik	निम्नवर्ग लिपिक

M

Magna Carta	mahaadhikar patra	महाधिकार पत्र
Maintenances Officer	sanrakshan adhikaaree	संरक्षण अधिकारी
Managing Committee	prabandh samiti	प्रबंध समिति
Maternity & child Welfare Centre	prasuti tathaa shishu kalyaan kendra	प्रसूति तथा शिशु कल्याण केंद्र
Mayor	nigmaadhyaksh, mahaapaali-kaadhyaksh	निगमाध्यक्ष, महापालिकाध्यक्ष
Mechanical Engineer	yaantrik abhiyantaa	यांत्रिक अभियंता
Medical Officer	chikitsaa adhikaaree	चिकित्सा अधिकारी
Military prisoner	sainik bandee	सैनिक बंदी
Ministerial service	mantrivargeeya sevaa	मंत्रिवर्गीय सेवा
Minister-in-charge	kaaryabhaaree mantree	कार्यभारी मंत्री
Minister of Agriculture	krishi mantree	कृषि मंत्री
Minister of Development	vikaas mantree	विकास मंत्री
Minister of Excise	aabkaaree mantree	आबकारी मंत्री
Minister of Finance	vitt mantree	वित्त मंत्री

Minister of Food	khaadya mantree	खाद्य मंत्री
Miscarrige of Justice	nyaaya kee hatyaa	न्याय की हत्या
M.L.A.	sadasya vidhaan sabhaa	सदस्य विधान सभा
M.L.C.	sadasya vidhaan parishad	सदस्य विधान परिषद
M.P.	sadasya lok sabhaa	सदस्य लोक सभा

N

National airway	raashtriya vaayu path	राष्ट्रीय वायु-पथ
National Cader Corps	raashtriya chhaatra senaa	राष्ट्रीय छात्र सेना
National highway	raashtriya raajpath	राष्ट्रीय राजपथ
Nationalization	raashtriyakaran	राष्ट्रीयकरण
Nation-builder	raashtranirmaataa	राष्ट्र-निर्माता
Non-gazetted	araajpatrit	अराजपत्रित
Nutrition Officer	poshan adhikaari	पोषण अधिकारी

O

Oath of allegiance	raajyanishthaa saapath	राज्यनिष्ठा शपथ
Office-bearer	padadhaaree	पदधारी
Office copy	kaaryaalay pratilipi	कार्यालय प्रतिलिपि
Officer-in-charge	kaaryaabhaaree/ prabhaaree	कार्यभारी/प्रभारी
Office superintendent	kaaryaalay adheekshak	कार्यालय अधीक्षक
Official language	rajbhaashaa	राजभाषा
Official liquidator	aayakaranaadhikaaree	आयकरणाधिकारी
Open session	khulaa adhiveshan	खुला अधिवेशन

English	Transliteration	Hindi
Opium deptt.	apheem vibhaag	अफीम विभाग
Opposition party	vipakshee	विपक्षी
Ordinance depot	aayudh aagaar	आयुध आगार
Outdoor patient	bahirvaasee rogee	बहिर्वासी रोगी
Outstanding accounts	ashodhit lekhaa	अशोधित लेखा

P

English	Transliteration	Hindi
Parliament	sansad	संसद
Parliamentarian	sansad sadasya	संसद सदस्य
Parliamentary Secretary	sansad sachiv	संसद सचिव
Peon-Book	preshya-pustikaa	प्रेष्य-पुस्तिका
Personal assistant	vaiyaktik sahaayak	वैयक्तिक सहायक
Pilot scheme	nabhpath-darshak yojna	नभपथदर्शक योजना
Planning Officer	niyojan adhikaaree	नियोजन अधिकारी
Planary session	sampoorn satra	सम्पूर्ण सत्र
Police Force	aarakshak dal	आरक्षक दल
Police station	thana	थाना
Polling booth	matdaan kendra	मतदान केन्द्र
Polling station	nirvaachan adhishthaan	निर्वाचन अधिष्ठान
Press communique	patra vigyapti	पत्र विज्ञप्ति
Press conference	patrakaar sammelan	पत्रकार सम्मेलन
Prime Minister	pradhaan mantree	प्रधान मंत्री
Proprietary body	swaamitv sansthaa	स्वामित्व संस्था
Provident Fund	purvopaayee kosh	पूर्वोपायी कोष
Provincial Government	praanteeya sarkaar	प्रान्तीय सरकार

Public health	jan swaasthya	जन स्वास्थ्य
Publicity Officer	prachaar adhikaaree	प्रचार अधिकारी
Public Prosecutor	shaaskeeya abhiyoktaa	शासकीय अभियोक्ता
Public Relations	lok sampark	लोक संपर्क
Officers	adhikaaree	अधिकारी
Public servants	jansewak	जनसेवक
Public Service Commission	jan sewaa aayog	जन सेवा आयोग
P.W.D.	lok nirmaan vibhaag	लोक-निर्माण विभाग

Q

Ouasi-judicial	ardhanyaayik	अर्ध-न्यायिक
Quasi-permanent	ardhasthaayee	अर्धस्थायी
Queen-mother	raajmaataa	राजमाता
Queen Regent	raajranee	राजरानी
Quorum	kaaryavaah sankhyaa	कार्यवाह संख्या

R

Radio talk	aakaashvaanee vaartaa	आकाशवाणी वार्ता
Railway administration	relmaarg prashaasan	रेलमार्ग प्रशासन
Rank and file	saadhaaran sainik varga	साधारण सैनिक वर्ग
Record-keeper	abhilekhpaal	अभिलेखपाल
Reference clerk	abhyuddesh lipik	अभ्युद्देश लिपिक
Refugee camp	sharanaarthee shivir	शरणार्थी शिविर

Refugee Liasion Officer	sharnaarthee sampark adhikaaree	शरणार्थी संपर्क अधिकारी
Regional Accounts Officer	praadeshik ganan adhikaaree	प्रादेशिक गणन अधिकारी
Regional Transport Authority	praadeshik vaahan praadhikaree	प्रादेशिक वाहन प्राधिकारी
Relieving Officer	mochak adhikaaree	मोचक अधिकारी
Republic	ganraajya, gantantra, jantantra	गणराज्य, गणतंत्र, जनतंत्र
Rural Development Deptt.	graam-sudhaar vibhaag	ग्राम-सुधार विभाग

S

Sales tax	bikree kar	बिक्री कर
Sanitary Inspector	aarogya swaasthya nireekshak	आरोग्य स्वास्थ्य निरीक्षक
Secondary Education	maadhyamik shikshaa	माध्यमिक शिक्षा
Secretary, Deputy	pratisachiv	प्रतिसचिव
Secretary of States	raajmantree	राजमंत्री
Secretary, Under	avar sachiva	अवर सचिव
Secular State	dharmnirapeksh raajya	धर्मनिरपेक्ष राज्य
Self-government	swaayatta shaasan	स्वायत्त शासन
Sessions Judge	dauraa jaj, satra nyaayaadheesh	दौरा जज, सत्र न्यायाधीश
Sine qua non	aparihaarya	अपरिहार्य
Sitting member	vidyamaan sadasya	विद्यमान सदस्य
Special audit	vishesh lekhaa	विशेष लेखा परीक्षा

	pareekshaaa	
Special messenger	vishesh dut	विशेष दूत
State funeral	rajya-sammaanit antyeshti	राज्य-सम्मानित अंत्येष्टि
Stenographer	aashulipik	आशुलिपिक
Supply and Disposals	sambharan va niptaan	संभरण व निपटान

T

T.A.	yaatra bhattaa	यात्रा भत्ता
Tariff	aayat-niryaat kar	आयात-निर्यात कर
Tax collector	kar samaahartaa	करसमाहर्ता
Technical branch	pravaidhik shaakhaa	प्रवैधिक शाखा
Tender form	nividaa patra	निविदा पत्र
Tenure of post	pad kee avadhi	पद की अवधि
Textile Industry	vastra-udyog	वस्त्र उद्योग
Time-keeper	samay-lekhak	समय-लेखक
Topographical maps	prishth-vivaran sambandhee nakshe	पृष्ठ-विवरण संबंधी नकशे
Transport Deptt.	parivahan vibhaag	परिवहन विभाग
Treasury Officer	koshaagaar adhikaaree	कोषागार अधिकारी
Tribunal Court	panch mandal	पंच मण्डल
Trust corporation	pranyaas nigam	प्रन्यास निगम

U

Under Secretary	awar sachiv	अवर सचिव
U.D.C.	uchch shrenee lipik	उच्च श्रेणी लिपिक
U.N.O.	sanyukta raashtra sangh	संयुक्त राष्ट्र संघ

V

Vacant possession	rikta bhoga	रिक्त भोग
Vaccination Act	teekaa adhiniyam	टीका अधिनियम
Valuation Act	moolyan vidhi	मूल्यन विधि
Venereal Deptt.	ratij rog vibhaag	रतिज रोग विभाग
Vested interest	nihit swaaratha	निहित स्वार्थ
Vice-Chancellor	up-kulpati	उप-कुलपति
Village headman	mukhiyaa	मुखिया
Visitors' gallery	darshak deerdhaa	दर्शक दीर्घा
Vocational staff	vyavasaayik	व्यवसायिक
	karmcharee varga	कर्मचारी वर्ग

W

Wage-earner	bhriti arjan	भृति अर्जन
	karnewaalaa	करनेवाला
Warrant Officer	waarant adhikaaree	वारंट अधिकारी
Welfare Officer	kalyaan adhikaaree	कल्याण अधिकारी
Whip	sachetak	सचेतक
Wireless operator	betaar prachaalak	बेतार प्रचालक
Works Manager	nirmaankaarya	निर्माणकार्य प्रबंधक
	prabandhak	

X

X-ray	ksha-rashmi	क्ष-राश्मि
X-ray deptt.	ksha-rashmi vibhaag	क्ष-राश्मि विभाग
X-ray room	ksha-rashmi koshtha	क्ष-राश्मि कोष्ठ

III FOREIGN WORDS USED IN ENGLISH

Boutique (Fr.)	dukaan	दुकान
Bravo (Fr.)	shaabaash	शाबाश
Coiffeur (Fr.)	baal sanwaarne-waalaa	बाल संवारने वाला
De jure(L.)	kaanunan	कानूनन
Detenue (Fr.)	kaidee	कैदी
Elite (Fr.)	uttam ansh	उत्तम अंश
Spouse (Fr.)	patnee	पत्नी
Ex officio (L.)	padaadhikaaren	पदाधिकारेण
Ibid (L.)	usee sthaan men	उसी स्थान में
Locus standi (L.)	hastakshep karne kaa adhikaar	हस्तक्षेप करने का अधिकार
Par excellence (Fr.)	shreshthataa/ khyaati se	श्रेष्ठता/ख्याति से
Per annum (L.)	prativarsha	प्रतिवर्ष
Per centum (L.)	prati saikraa	प्रति सैकड़ा
Per diem (L.)	pratidin	प्रतिदिन
Per se (L.)	swayam	स्वयं
Prima facie (L.)	pahlee drishti men	पहली दृष्टि में
Pro rata (L.)	anupaat men	अनुपात में
Sine die (L.)	anishchit kaal ke liye sthagit	अनिश्चित काल के लिए स्थगित
Sine qua non (L.)	anivaarya sthiti	अनिवार्य स्थिति
Sub judice (L.)	vichaaraadheen	विचाराधीन
Via (L.)	raaste se	रास्ते से
Vice (L.)	badle men	बदले में
Vice versa (L.)	shabda kaa kram	शब्द का क्रम उलटा हुआ

| Vis-a-vis (Fr.) | aamne saamne | आमने-सामने |
| Viva-voce (L.) | maukhik pareekshaa se | मौखिक परीक्षा से |

IV TELEGRAPHIC GREETINGS

1. Wish you a happy new year	Navavarsh kee shubhkaam-naayen	नववर्ष की शुभकामनाएं
2. Many happy returns of the day	Iswar kare yah shubh din baar baar aawe	ईश्वर करे यह शुभ दिन बार-बार आवे
3. Wish you merry X'mas	Baraa din mubaarak	बड़ा दिन मुबारक
4. Id mubarak	Id mubaarak	ईद मुबारक
5. May God bless-your new born son	Bhagvaan kare tumhaaraa navjaat shishu phoole-phale	भगवान करे तुम्हारा नवजात शिशु फूले-फले
6. May God bless you recovery	Bhagwaan tumhen aarogya pradaan kare	भगवान तुम्हें आरोग्य प्रदान करे
7. Heartfelt congratulations on your winning distinction	Tumhaaree vishishtataa par meree haardik badhaaee	तुम्हारी विशिष्टता पर मेरी हार्दिक बधाई
8. Heartiest congratulations on your winning the lottery	Lautaree kee jeet par haardik badhaaee	लाटरी की जीत पर हार्दिक बधाई
9. Wish you a happy conjugal life	Sukhmay daampatya jeevan kee shubhkaamnaayen	सुखमय दामपत्य जीवन की शुभकामनाएं

| 10. My heartiest Diwali greetings | Diwalee kee shubhkaamnaayen | दिवाली की शुभकामनाएं |
| 11. Many thanks for your good wishes | Tumhaaree shubhkaamnaaaon ke liye bahut bahut dhanyavaad | तुम्हारी शुभकामनाओं के लिये बहुत बहुत धन्यवाद |

V SHORT LETTERS

1. Application for casual leave

Sir,

   I have the honour to state that I am feeling feverish. I'd, therefore, request you to please grant me casual leave for today.

          Thanking you,

                              Yours faithfully,

मान्यवर महोदय,

   सेवा में निवेदन है कि मुझे आज बुखार-सा महसूस हो रहा है । अतः आप से अनुरोध है कि आप मुझे आज की आकस्मिक छुट्टी मंजूर करने की कृपा करें ।

      सधन्यवाद,

                              भवदीय

Maanyavar Mahoday,

   Sewaa men nivedan hai ki mujhe aaj bukhaar-saa mahsoos ho rahaa hai. Atah aapse anurodh hai ki aap mujhe aaj kee aakasmik chhuttee manjur karne kee kripaa karen.

      Sadhanyavaad,

                              Bhavadeeya,

2. Application for earned leave

Sir,

I have the honour to bring to your kind notice that my brother's marriage is going to be held and I have to arrange the ceremony. So I won't be able to do my duty for a fortnight with effect from.....to.....

I, therefore, request you to kindly grant me earned leave for that period.

Thanking you,

Yours faithfully,

माननीय महोदय,

सेवा में सूचित करना चाहता हूँ कि मेरे भाई की शादी होने जा रही है और मुझे समारोह का प्रबन्ध करना है। अतः मैं ता०.............से..........तक अपनी डिऊटी पर नहीं आ सकूंगा।

अतः मैं आपसे गुजारिश करूँगा कि आप मेरी उक्त अवधि की अर्जित छुट्टी मंजूर करने की कृपा करेंगे।

सधन्यवाद,

भवदीय

Maanneeya Mahoday,

Sewaa men soochit karnaa chahaataa hoon ki mere bhaaee kee shaadee hone jaa rahee hai aur mujhe samaaroh kaa prabandh karnaa hai. Atah main taareekh...........se..........tak apnee diutee par naheen aa sakoongaa.

Atah main aapse gujaarish karoongaa ki aap meri ukt awadhi kee arjit chhuttee manjoor karne kee kripaa karen.

Sadhanyavaad,

Bhavadeeya,

3. Invitation to dinner

Dear Prem,

Tonight we are going to celebrate our son's birthday. Hence we take the privilege to extend our invitation to you at dinner on the auspiciouus occasion.

Hope you will grace the occasion and bless your nephew.

Yours sincerely,

प्रिय प्रेम,

आज हम अपने सुपुत्र का जन्म-दिवस मनाने जा रहे हैं। चुनांचे हम तुम्हें इस शुभ अवसर पर भोज पर आमंत्रित करने का सौभाग्य प्राप्त कर रहे हैं।

आशा है, तुम उपस्थित होकर इस समारोह की शोभा बढ़ाओगे और अपने भतीजे को आशीर्वाद दोगे।

तुम्हारा,

Priya Prem,

Aaj ham apne suputra kaa janm-divas manaane jaa rahe hain. Chunaache ham tumhen is shubh avasar par bhoj par aamantrit karne kaa saubhagya praapt kar rahe hain.

Aasha hai, tum upasthit hokar is samaaroh kee shobhaa barhaavoge aur apne bhateeje ko aashirvad doge.

Tumhaaraa,

4. Placing order for books

Dear Sirs,

I need badly two books—*Pilgrims Progress* by Gladstone and *Destiny* by Baniyan. Hence, I'd request you to kindly send me these by V.P.P. at your earliest.

Thanking you,

Yours faithfully,

प्रिय महोदय,

मुझे दो पुस्तकों की सख्त जरूरत है 'पिलग्रिम्स प्रोग्रेस' द्वारा ग्लैडस्टोन और 'डेसिटनी' द्वारा बनियान। चुनांचे मैं आपसे निवेदन करूँगा कि आप इन्हें यथाशीघ्र वी०पी०पी० द्वारा भेज दें।

सधन्यवाद,

भवदीय,

Maanyavar Mahoday,

Mujhe do pustakon kee sakht jarurat hai—*Pilgrims prosgress* dwaaraa Gladstone aur *Destinee* dwaaraa Buniyan. Chunaanche main aapse nivedan karoongaa ki aap inhen yathaasheeghra vee.pee.pee.dwaaraa bhej den.

    Sadhanyavaad,

                      Bhavadeeya,

PART 4
Conversations

1. MEETING & PARTING

1. Good morning, Sir	Namaste mahaashayjee	नमस्ते, महाशय जी
2. Good morning, gentleman	Namaste, sajjan	नमस्ते, सज्जन
3. You are from England	Aap inglaind se aaye hain	आप इंग्लैंड से आए हैं
4. Yes	jee haan	जी हां
5. On a visit to India?	Bhaarat bhraman ke liye?	भारत भ्रमण के लिए?
6. Of course	Beshak	बेशक
7. You need a tourist guide?	Aap ko turist gaaid kee zarurat hai?	आपको टूरिस्ट गाइड की जरूरत है?
8. O Yes!	jee haan	जी हां !
9. Here I am at men your service.	Main aap kee sewaa mai haazir hoon.	मैं आपकी सेवा में हाजिर हूँ,
10. Thank you	Dhanyavaad.	धन्यवाद
11. You'd like to put up in a hotel?	Aap kisee hotal men thaharnaa	आप किसी होटल में ठहरना पसंद करेंगे

	pasand karenge?	
12. Yes, in a nice one	Haan, kisee achche hotal mein	हाँ, किसी अच्छे होटल में
13. Ashoka is the best	Ashoka sabse achchhaa hai	अशोक सबसे अच्छा है
14. I've heard of it	Maine iske baare men sunaa hai	मैंने इसके बारे में सुना है
15. It has all the amenities	Ismen saaree suvidhaayen hain	इसमें सारी सुविधाएं हैं
16. Good' then	Achchhaa hai tab	अच्छा है तब
17. Foreigners like it	Videshee ise pasand karte hain	विदेशी इसे पसंद करते हैं
18. I, too, will like it then	Main bhee tab pasand karoongaa	मैं भी तब पसन्द करूँगा
19. May I take you there?	Main aapko vahaan le chaloon?	मैं आपको वहां ले चलूं
20. Yes	Haan	हाँ
21. Here is the Ashoka	Yah rahaa ashok	यह रहा अशोक
22. It's magnificent	Yah shaandaar hai	यह शानदार है
23. Single room will do?	Ek kamre se kaam chalegaa?	एक कमरे से काम चलेगा?
24. No, double room	Naheen, do kamre	नही, दो कमरे
25. For how many days?	Kitne dinon ke liye?	कितने दिनों के लिए?
26. For a fortnight	Pakwaare ke liye.	पखवारे के लिए
27. Here are the rooms	Ye rahe kamre	ये रहे कमरे
28. With all the amenities. Good	Saaree suvidhya hain. Achchhaa hai	सारी सुविधाएं हैं, अच्छा है
29. May I leave	Sir, ab	सर, अब

	now, Sir?	main chaloon	मैं चलूँ
30.	After having a cup of coffee	Ek kap kauphee peekar	एक कप कॉफी पीकर
31.	Would you need my service tomorrow?	Kal aap ko meree sewaa kee zaroorat hogee?	कल आपको मेरी सेवा की जरूरत होगी?
32.	Yes, to take me around the city	Haan, mujhko shahar ghumaaneke liye	हाँ, मुझको शहर घुमाने के लिए
33.	Thank you for the coffee	Kauphee ke liyae dhanyavaad	कॉफी के लिए धन्यवाद
34.	And thank you for your help	Aur madad ke liye aapko dhanyavaad	और मदद के लिए आपको धन्यवाद

II PLEASING & SURPRISING

1.	Where is Peter? In his room	Peetar kahaan hai? Apne kamre men	पीटर कहां है? अपने कमरे में
2.	Well, my boy! Yes, daddy!	Mere bete! Jee, pitaajee !	मेरे बेटे जी, पिताजी
3.	I'm very pleased today It's good	Aaj main bahut khush hoon Yah achchhee baat hai	आज मैं बहुत खुश हूँ यह अच्छी बात है
4.	You know why ? I don't know	Tum jaante ho kyon? Main naheen jaantaa.	तुम जानते हो, क्यों? मैं नही जानता
5.	You are my pride, son. How so?	Tum mere gaurav ho, putra. Wah kaise?	तुम मेरे गौरव हो, पुत्र वह कैसे?
6.	You've brought pride to my family.	Tumne mere kul ko gaurav pardan kia hai	तुमने मेरे कुल को गौरव प्रदान किया है।

I don't know how	Main naheen jaantaa kaise	मैं नहीं जानता कैसे
7. You've secured Honours in English, Really?	Tumne angrezee men aunars haasil kiyaa. hai Sachmuch?	तुमने अंगरेज़ी में ऑनर्स हासिल किया है, सचमुच?
8. Really...And dsitinction too. True, daddy?	Sachmuch... aur vishishtata bhee. Sachmuch, pitajee?	सचमुच... और विशिष्टता भी, सचमुच, पिताजी ?
9. True, boy. And my joy knows no bounds. My joy, too.	Sachmuch, beta Aur meree khushee kee seemaa nahin hai. Meree khushee kee bhee	सचमुच, बेटा...और मेरी खुशी की सीमा नहीं है मेरी खुशी की भी
10. And mine as well, my son, It's all by your grace, mom	Sath hee meree bhee mere putra. Yah sab tumhaaraa aashirvad hai, maan	और साथ ही मेरी भी, मेरे पुत्र, यह सब तुम्हारा आशीर्वाद है, माँ
11. Annie dear, arrange a pompous dinner tonight Ha, let me first go to the church.	Ennee priye! aaj raat shaandaar khaanaa banaao Theek hai, mujhko pahle girjaa jaane do.	एन्नी प्रिये ! आज रात शानदार खाना बनाओ ठीक है, मुझको पहले गिरजा जाने दो
12. Mom, I will also go. Come on, boy	Maan ! main bhee chaloonga Aa jao, mere bete.	माँ ! मैं भी चलूंगा आ जाओ, मेरे बेटे !

III ANGER & BLAME

1. Where is Daisy? I don't know	Desee kahaan hai? Main naheen jaantee	डेज़ी कहां है? मैं नहीं जानती

2. You're her mom and you don't know? — Tum uskee maan ho aur naheen jaantee? — तुम उसकी मां हो और नहीं जानती ?

You mean I should keep on guarding her? — Tumhaaraa matlab main uskee choksee kartee rahoon? — तुम्हारा मतलब मैं उसकी चौकसी करती रहूँ

3. But you must not set her free — Lekin tumhen use aajaad naheen chhor denaa hai. — लेकिन तुम्हें उसे आजाद नहीं छोड़ देना है।

Should I keep her in the cage? — Kyaa main use pinjare men band rakhoon? — क्या मैं उसे पिंजड़े में बंद रखूँ !

4. Will you let flirt around then? — Kyaa tum use aawaargee karne ke liye chhor dogee? — क्या तुम उसे आवारगी करने के लिए छोड़ दोगी ?

What has bitten you today? — Aaj tumko ho kyaa gayaa hai? — आज तुमको हो क्या गया है ?

5. Snake has bitten me — Saanp ne kaata hai. — सांप ने काटा है
It looks like that. — Aisaa hee lagtaa hai. — ऐसा ही लगता है

6. I'll strangle her today. — Aaj main uskaa galaa ghont dungaa — आज मैं उसका गला घोंट दूंगा,
But why? — Par kyon? — पर क्यों ?

7. She has brought me blame. — Usne mujhko badnaam kiyaa hai. — उसने मुझको बदनाम किया है
Blame? How? — Badnaam? Kaise? — बदनाम? कैसे?

8. She has conceived — Usne garbh dhaaran kiyaa hai. — उसने गर्भ धारण किया है।

Who told you? — Tumse kisne kahaa? — तुमसे किसने कहा ?

9. My doctor friend. And how could he know?

Mere dauktar mitra ne. Aur usko kaise maaloom?

मेरे डॉक्टर मित्र ने। और उसको कैसे मालूम ?

10. She had gone to him. For what?

Wah uske paas gaee thee. Kisliye?

वह उसके पास गई थी। किसलिए?

11. For medicine, For getting abortion.

Davaa ke liye. Garbhpaat ke liye.

दवा के लिए, गर्भपात के लिए!

12. Yes. No matter

Han. Koee harj naheen.

हाँ कोई हर्ज नही

13. My reputation is at stake.... and no harm? Everthing will come round. Don't worry at trifles.

Meree badnaamee ho rahee hai... aur koee baat naheen? Sab kuchh theek ho jaayagaa. Tuchchh baat ke liye ghabraao naheen.

मेरी बदनामी हो रही है...और कोई बात नहीं ? सब कुछ ठीक हो जाएगा, तुच्छ बात के लिए घबराओ नहीं।

14. All this is trifle? Yes...in these days.

Yah sab kuchh tuchchh baat hai? Haan...aaj ke jamaane men.

यह सब कुछ तुच्छ बात है ? हाँ... आज के जमाने में

IV BED TEA

1. Good morning, dear Good morning, sweety

namaste, priye! Namaste, jaaneman!

नमस्ते, प्रिये ! नमस्ते, जानेमन !

2. Have bed tea Thank you

chay piyo shukriya

चाय पीयो शुक्रिया

3. It's nice?

Achchee hai?

अच्छी है ?

Yes,..and you are nicer	Haan achchee hai... par tum isase bhi jyaadaa achchee ho.	हां, अच्छी है.... तुम इससे भी ज्यादा अच्छी हो
4. It's hot. And you are hotter.	Yah garm hai. Tum isase bhee garm ho.	यह गरम है। तुम इससे भी गरम हो।
5. Its having flavours. Isn't?	Ismen sugandh hai... na	इसमें सुगंध है, है न?
It is and you having more fragrance.	Hai...par tumamen isase barhkar sugandh hai	है, पर तुममें इससे बढ़कर सुगंध है।
6. One should learn from you how to praise.	Taareef karnaa koyee tumse seekhe	तारिफ करना कोई तुमसे सीखे
Beauty deserves praise.	Sundartaa taareef ke kaabil hoti hai.	सुंदरता तारीफ के काबिल होती है

V. BREAKFAST

1. John—The breakfast is light	John, Naastaa halka hai	जॉन, नाश्ता हल्का है
2. Tom—And you like a heavy one	Tom, Aur tumko bhaaree pasand hai	टॉम-और तुमको भारी पसंद है
3. Dad—He is an athlete. That's why.	Pitaa wah khilaree hai... isliye	पिता वह, खिलाड़ी है, इसलिए
4. Mom—He should have nutritious one	Mam Isko pushti-kaarak naastaa milnaa chaahiye.	माँ—इसको पुष्टि-कारक नाश्ता मिलना चाहिए
5. John—Yes...half boiled	Jaun han...aadhe uble	जॉन—हाँ...आधे उबले
eggs, and milk and fruits	ande, doodh aur phal.	अंडे, दूध और फल

6. Tom—And you get toast and butter only... and tea in place of milk

Taum—Aur tumko tost aur makkhan miltaa hai sirph... aur doodh kee jagah chay.

टॉम—और तुमको टोस्ट और मक्खन मिलता है सिर्फ... और दूध की जगह चाय।

7. Mom—We are poor. We can't afford heavy and nutritious breakfast.

Man—Ham gareeb hain. Ham pushti-kaarak aur bhaaree naastaa naheen muhaiyaa kar paate

माँ—हम गरीब हैं। हम पुष्टिकारक और भारी नाश्ता नहीं मुहैया कर पाते

8. Dad—I am the only earning member, a petty clerk

Pitaa—Sirph main hee ek kamaanewaalaa hun...ek saadhaaran kiraanee

पिता—सिर्फ मै ही एक कमाने वाला हूँ.... एक साधारण किरानी

9. Tom—Don't worry, dad, I shall start earning very soon

Taum—Ghabraaeeyee naheen pitaajee, main bahut jald kamaanaa shuru karoongaa

टॉम—घबराईये नही पिताजी, मैं बहुत जल्द कमाना शुरू करूँगा

10. Mom—And then we'll have better diets

Man—Aur tab ham behtar bhojan karange

माँ—और तब हम बेहतर भोजन करेंगे

VI LUNCH

1. It's 1.30

Derh baje hain.

डेढ़ बजे हैं

2. Time to take lunch

Khaane kaa samay ho gayaa hai

खाने का समय हो गया है

3. Let's have it

Chalo khaanaa khaayen

चलो खाना खायें

4. Ha, nice menu !

Waah ! majedaar khaanaa !

वाह ! मजेदार खाना !

5. I like korma

Main kormaa bahut

मै कोरमा बहुत

very much.	jyaadaa pasand kartaa hoon.	ज्यादा पसंद करता हूँ
6. Then eat to your fill	Tab bhar pet khaoo	तब भर पेट खाओ
7. Mom, you are a good cook.	Maan, tum achchhee rasoeeyaa ho	माँ, तुम अच्छी रसोईया हो
8. But your dad says I don't cook nice	Lekin tumhaare pitaajee kahte hain main achchhaa naheen pakaatee.	लेकिन तुम्हारे पिताजी कहते हैं मैं अच्छा नहीं पकाती
9. He jests	We majaak karte hain	वे मजाक करते हैं
10. He has cosmop- olitan taste	Uskaa swaad vishvagrihee hai.	उसका स्वाद विश्वगृही है
11. Because he travelled all round.	Choonki we ᶜhaaron or bhraman kiye hain	चूँकि वे चारों ओर भ्रमण किए हैं
12. Why don't you take the pudding?	Tum kheer kyon naheen khaate?	तुम खीर क्यों नहीं खाते ?
13. Ah, I forgot	Ah, main to bhool hee gayaa thaa	आह, मैं तो भूल ही गया था
14. How does it taste?	Kaisaa lagtaa hai yah?	कैसा लगता है यह ?
15. Sweet..so sweet	Meetha...bahut meetha!	मीठा....बहुत मीठा
16. There are pista- chioes in it.	Ismen piste dale hain	इसमें पिस्ते डले हैं

VII EVENING TEA

1. It's very cold today	Aaj bahut sardee hai.	आज बहुत सर्दी है
2. Let's ask mom to prepare 'pakaure'	Chalo maan se kahen pakaure banaane ko.	चलो मां से कहें पकौड़े बनाने को ।
3. And I'm going to have 'samose'.	Aur main samose laane jaa rahaa hoon.	और मैं समोसे लाने जा रहा हूँ

4. Bring eight pieces.

Aath laanaa.

आठ लाना

5. What about money?

Paise kahaan se aayenge?

पैसे कहां से आयेंगे ?

6. How much you have?

Tumhaare paas kitne hain?

तुम्हारे पास कितने हैं ?

7. Only five rupees.

Sirph paanch rupaye.

सिर्फ पांच रुपये

8. You need three more. Have these.

Tumko aur teen chaahiye. Yah lo.

तुमको और तीन चाहिए, यह लो

9. Give me two more.

Mujhko do aur do.

मुझको दो और दो

10. What for?

Kisliye?

किसलिए ?

11. For cigarettes.

Sigaret ke liye.

सिगरेट के लिए

12. Tea will do or coffee?

Chaay chalegee ya kaufee !

चाय चलेगी या कॉफी !

13. Coffee will be better.

Kaufee achchhee rahegee

कॉफी अच्छी रहेगी

VIII DINNER

1. Dear, isn't it time for dinner?

Preetam, bhojan kaa samay naheen huaa hai

प्रीतम, भोजन का समय नहीं हुआ है ?

2. Yes, it is... I'm coming.

Haan, ho gayaa hai.... main aa rahaa hoon.

हाँ, हो गया है...मैं आ रहा हूँ

3. Call Sanjay.

Sanjay ko aawaaz de do.

संजय को आवाज़ दे दो

4. Sanjay boy, join the dinner. Call Sunita.

Sanjay betaa, khaanaa khaa lo. Suneeta ko bulaa lo.

संजय बेटा, खाना खा लो सुनीता, को बुला लो

5. Ha, you've cooked so many items.

Ahaa, tumne to bahut se aaitams. banaaye hain

अहा, तुमने तो बहुत से आइटम्स बनाए हैं !

6. Chapaatees, rice,

Chapaatiyaan, chaawal,

चपातियां, चावल,

pulse, vegetable, pickles, papar, and curd.	daal, sabjee, achaar, paapar aur dahee.	दाल, सब्जी, अचार, पापड़ और दही ।
7. No sweet?	Koee meethaa naheen?	कोई मीठा नहीं ?
8. Ha, there are rasgullas. I just forgot to serve.	Are. Resgulle hain! main to bhool hee gayee thee parosanaa.	अरे....रसगुल्ले हैं ।... मैं तो भूल ही गई थी परोसना ।
9. Sunita baby, you don't help your mom in the kitchen?	Suneetaa betee, tum rasoee men maan kee madad naheen kartee?	सुनीता बेटी, तुम रसोई में मां की मदद नहीं करती ?
10. Mom doesn't allow me to cook. She wants me to read.	Maan mujhko anumati naheen deti. Wha chaahtee hai main parhoon.	माँ मुझको अनुमति नहीं देती वह चाहती है मैं पढ़ूँ
11. I'll look for a maid-servant to help her.	Main ek naukraanee kee talaash karunga iskee madad ke liya.	मैं एक नौकरानी की तलाश करूँगा इसकी मदद के लिए
12. Yes. She is too old.	Haan. Yah bahoot burhee ho gaee hai.	हाँ...यह बहुत बूढ़ी हो गई है ।
13. Dad, why don't you get Sanjay wedded?	Pitaajee, aap Sanjay kee shaadee kyon naheen kar dete?	पिताजी, आप संजय की शादी क्यों नहीं कर देते ?
14. If you do so, my daughter-in-law would manage the cooking.	Agar waisaa karte to meree bahu rasoee sambhaal letee.	अगर वैसा करते तो मेरी बहू रसोई संभाल लेती ।
15. I'm thinking over it.	Main is vishay men soch rahaa hoon.	मैं इस विषय में सोच रहा हूँ

IX STROLL

1. Let's go for a stroll	Chalo zaraa tahal aaen	चलो ज़रा टहल आएं
2. Where? No park nearby.	Kahaan? Paas men koee paark bhee to naheen hai.	कहां ? पास में कोई पार्क भी तो नहीं है ।
3. We'll stroll on the road.	Ham sarak par tahlenge	हम सड़क पर टहलेंगे
4. It's nonsense.	Bakvas hai.	बकवास
5. How?	Kyon?	क्यों?
6. Heavy traffic coming and going, din and bustle all round, dust and rubbles.	Bhaaree vaahan aate jaate hai charon or shoro-gul, dhul aur gard.	भारी वाहन आते जाते हैं चारों ओर... शोरो-गुल, धूल और गर्द
7. We'll go to Apollo	Hamlog apolo chalenge	हमलोग अपोलो चलेंगे
8. And have coffee.	Aur kaufee peeyenge.	और कॉफी पिएंगे ।
9. Yes.	Han.	हाँ

X VISIT

1. It's too hot.	Bahut garmee hai.	बहुत गर्मी है
2. Because it is August.	Choonki yah agast kaa maheenaa hai	चूँकि यह अगस्त का महीना है
3. August is the hottest month?	Agast kyaa sabse garm maheenaa hai?	अगस्त क्या सबसे गर्म महीना है ?
4. Yes...in Delhi.	Haan....dillee mein.	हाँ.....दिल्ली में
5. Ah, it's unbearable.	Aah, yah asahya hai.	आह, यह असह्य है
6. And no aircooler.	Uparse eyar kular bhee naheen.	ऊपर से एयर कूलर भी नहीं

7. Electricity also very often fails.	Bijlee bhee bahut baar naheen hotee hai.	बिजली भी बहुत बार नहीं होती है
8. I'm thinking to go on a visit	Main sair par jaane kee soch rahaa hoon.	मैं सैर पर जाने की सोच रहा हूँ
9. Where?	Kahan?	कहाँ?
10. Mussouri.	Masooree.	मसूरी।
11. For how many days?	Kitne dinon ke liye?	कितने दिनों के लिए ?
12. A couple of months.	Do maheenon ke liye.	दो महीनों के लिए
13. Mussouri is a hill station. You will enjoy it.	Masuree paharee jagah hai. Tum iskaa aanand loge.	मसूरी पहाड़ी जगह है, तुम इसका आनंद लोगे।
14. Why don't you accompany me?	Tum kyon naheen mere saath chalte?	तुम क्यों नहीं मेरे साथ चलते ?
15. I won't get leave.	Mujhko chhuttee naheen milegee.	मुझको छुट्टी नहीं मिलेगी
16. So what? At the most you won't get your pay.	To kyaa huaa? Yahee hogaa naa ki tumko tankhaah naheen milegee.	तो क्या हुआ ? यही होगा न कि तुमको तनखाह नहीं मिलेगी
17. But I can't do without it.	Lakin iske binaa mera kaam chalne kaa naheen.	लेकिन इसके बिना मेरा काम चलने का नहीं
18. But I can't enjoy with-out you.	Lekin mujhko tere binaa aanand naheen aayegaa.	लेकिन मुझको तेरे बिना आनंद नहीं आयेगा
19. Then let's pay a short visit.	Tab hamlog kuchh dinon ke liye chalen	तब हमलोग कुछ दिनों के लिए चलें
20. For a fortnight at least.	Kam se kam ek pakhwaare ke liye	कम से कम एक पखवारे के लिए

XI INVITATION

1. It's an invitation letter.	Yah nimantran patra hai.	यह निमंत्रण पत्र है
2. Wherefrom?	Kahaan se?	कहां से ?
3. From Muradabad.	Muradabad se.	मुरादाबाद से
4. Your friend Sanjiv's?	Tumhaare dost Sanjeev ke yahaan se?	तुम्हारे दोस्त संजीव के यहां से ?
5. Yes, he is going to be married.	Han. Uskee shaadee hone jaa rahee hai.	हाँ....उसकी शादी होने जा रही है
6. When?	Kab?	कब ?
7. On this tenth.	Isee dasween taareekh ko.	इसी दसवीं तारीख को
8. It is seventh today.	Aaj saatween hai.	आज सातवीं है
9. Our presence is earnestly solicited.	Hamaaree upasthiti prarthaneeya hai	हमारी उपस्थिति प्रार्थनीय है
10. You must go then.	Tab tumko awashya jaanaa chaahiye.	तब तुमको अवश्य जाना चाहिए
11. You too.	Tumko bhee.	तुमको भी
12. He has invited me?	Usne mujhko aamantrit kiyaa hai?	उसने मुझको आमंत्रित किया है ?
13. Just read it.	Isko parhkar dekho.	इसको पढ़कर देखो....
14. We have to buy the present then.	Hamen tab uphaar khareednaa hogaa.	हमें तब उपहार खरीदना होगा
15. The gift should be a nice one.	Uphaar uttam honaa chaahiye.	उपहार उत्तम होना चाहिए
16. Let's go to the market and choose.	Chalo baazaar chalkar chunen.	चलो, बाज़ार चलकर चुनें

XII TRAVEL

English	Transliteration	Hindi
1. Drive me to the station.	Mujhe steshan le chalo.	मुझे स्टेशन ले चलो....
2. Ah, you're very slow.	Aah, tum bahut dheeme chalaate ho.	आह, तुम बहुत धीमे चलाते हो....
3. I have to reach latest by 6.30.	Saarhe chhah tak mujhko pahunchnaa hee hai.	साढ़े छः तक मुझको पहुंचना ही है
4. Don't worry, please. I'll get you there before time.	Kripayaa ghabraaiye naheen, main aap ko samay se pahle pahunchaa doongaa.	कृपया घबराइये नहीं, मैं आपको समय से पहले पहुंचा दूंगा
5. Thank you, driver. How much should I pay you?	Driver, tumko dhanyavaad. Kitnaa doon tumhen?	ड्राइवर, तुमको धन्यवाद, कितना दूं तुम्हें ?
6. Only twenty rupees.	Sirph bees rupaye.	सिर्फ बीस रुपए
7. Have it.	Yah lo.	यह लो
8. Thank you.	Aapko dhanyavaad.	आपको धन्यवाद
9. Coolie, carry these to platform no. 7.	Kulee, inhen pletfaarm namber saat me le jaao.	कूली, इन्हें प्लेटफार्म नं. सात में ले जाओ
10. Ramesh, you accompany him.	Ramesh, tum iske saath jaao.	रमेश, तुम इसके साथ जाओ
11. I'm going to have tickets.	Main tikaten lene jaa rahaa hoon.	मैं टिकटें लेने जा रहा हूँ...
12. Two tickets IInd class, Mumbai	Do tikaten, doosree shrenee, Mumbai.	दो टिकटें, दूसरी श्रेणी, मुंबई
13. Thank God, we are in time. Ramesh	Shukra bhagvaan kaa, ham samay par	शुक्र भगवान का, हम समय पर

	it's big rush.	pahunch gaye. Ramesh, bahut bheer hai.	पहुंच गये। रमेश, बहुत भीड़ है।
14.	Ah, very trouble-some to get in.	Aaha ghusnaa baraa kashtkar hai.	आ घुसना बड़ा कष्टकर है
15.	The compartment is packed to its capacity	Dibbaa khachakhach bharaa hai.	डिब्बा खचाखच भरा है
16.	Thank God, we got in.	Dhanya bhaagya, ham ghus gaye.	धन्य भाग्य, हम घुस गए
17.	Our luggage is allright?	Hamaaraa saamaan theek hai?	हमारा समान ठीक है?
18.	Allright.	Theek hai.	ठीक है
19.	See the condition of the compartment.	Dibbe kee haalat dekho	डिब्बे की हालत देखो
20.	So dirty it is !	Kitnaa gandaa hai yah!	कितना गंदा है यह!
21.	How long we'll remain standing?	Ham kitnee der khare rahenge!	हम कितनी देर खड़े रहेंगे?
22.	Oh, I'll be tired.	Aah, main thak jaoongaa.	आह, मैं थक जाऊंगा
23.	See these hawkers.	In phereewaalon ko dekho.	इन फेरीवालों को देखो
24.	They create nuisance.	Ye klesh utpanna karte hain.	ये क्लेश उत्पन्न करते हैं
25.	They are a headache.	Ye sirdard hain.	ये सिरदर्द हैं
26.	The guard whistled.	Gaard ne seetee bajaaee.	गार्ड ने सीटी बजाई
27.	The train steamed off.	Gaaree chal dee	गाड़ी चल दी
28.	See its fast speed.	Iskee tej raftaar dekho.	इसकी तेज रफ्तार देखो
29.	It is superfast.	Yah supar fast hai.	यह सुपर फास्ट है

XIII HOTEL

1. Darling, have you ever seen a caberet?	Priye, tumne kabhee kaibre (naach) dekhaa hai?	प्रिये, तुमने कभी कैब्रे (नाच) देखा है ?
2. No, dear.	Naheen pyare.	नहीं प्यारे
3. Get ready, I'll show you	Taiyaar ho jaao, main tumhen dikhaa laaun.	तैयार हो जाओ, मैं तुम्हें दिखा लाऊं
4. In the Park Hotel?	Paark hotel mein?	पार्क होटल में?
5. Yes, it's one of the best hotels.	Haan, yah sabse sundar hotlon me ek hai.	हां, यह सबसे सुंदर होटलों में एक है
6. The caberet is nice or not?	Kaibre sundar hotaa hai yaa naheen?	कैब्रे सुंदर होता है या नहीं ?
7. It is very nice.	Sundar hota hai.	सुंदर होता है
8. We'll take there dinner too?	Hamlog wahaan khaanaa bhee khaayenge?	हम लोग वहां खाना भी खायेंगे ?
9. Sure...tandoori chicken.	Zaroor. Tanduree chicken.	जरूर...तंदूरी चिकेन
10. I've heard much of its shaamee kabaab.	Maine iske shaamee kabab kee baree taareef sunee hai.	मैंने इसके शामी कबाब की बड़ी तारीफ सुनी है ।
11. We'll take that too?	Hum use bhee khaayenge.	हम उसे भी खायेंगे
12. You'll drink too?	Tum peeyoge bhee?	तुम पियोगे भी?
13. A little, a peg or two.	Thoree see, ek ya do peg.	थोड़ी सी, एक या दो पेग..
14. Not more?	Jyaadaa naheen?	ज्यादा नहीं?
15. No.	Naheen.	नहीं

16. Swear on me?	Meree kasam?	मेरी कसम
17. Swear on you.	Tumhaaree kasam.	तुम्हारी कसम
18. Good evening, Sir and Madam.	Namaste huzoor aur mohtarmaa.	नमस्ते हुज़ूर और मोहतरमा
19. Good evening.	Namaste.	नमस्ते....
20. Waiter.	Bairaa...	बैरा....
21. Yes, Sir.	Jee huzoor.	जी हुज़ूर....
22. A peg of scotch whiskey	Skoch whiskee kaa ek peg.	स्कॉच हिसकी का एक पेग
23. Chicken soup for me.	Cheeken soop mere liye.	चिकेन सूप मेरे लिए
24. See the caberet.	kaibre dekho.	कैब्रे देखो
25. Ha, she dances so nice.	Wah. Sunder naachtee hai vah.	वाह...सुंदर नाचती है वह
26. But very shameless she is.	Lekin bahut besharm hai vah.	लेकिन बहुत बेशर्म है वह..
27. Because she is naked?	Choonki vah nagna hai?	चूंकि वह नग्न हैं ?
28. Yes.	Haan.	हाँ
29. Waiter, another peg for me and shaami kabaab for memsaaheb.	Bairaa, mere liye doosraa peg aur memsaaheb ke liye shaamee kabaab.	बैरा, मेरे लिए दूसरा पेग और मेम साहब के लिए शामी कबाब
30. No peg now, remember?	Ab aur peg naheen, yaad hai na?	अब और पेग नहीं, याद है न
31. I remember.	Mujhko yaad hai.	मुझको याद है....

XIV PURCHASE

| 1. This is Palika bazar. | Yah paalikaa baazaar hai. | यह पालिका बाज़ार है |
| 2. It is underground. | Yah underground hai. | यह अंडरग्राउन्ड है |

3. The best shopping centre.	Sabse achchhaa khareed kendra.	सबसे अच्छा खरीद केन्द्र
4. Ha, so many shops!	Waah, kitnee dukaanen hain.	वाह, कितनी दुकानें हैं!
5. And with varieties!	Aur vividhtaa liye!	और विविधता लिए !
6. I'll buy a few shirts.	Main kuchh kameejen khareedoongaa.	मैं कुछ कमीज़ें खरीदूंगा
7. And I'll buy blouses	Aur main blaooj khareedoongee.	और मैं ब्लाउज़ खरीदूंगी
8. Have a look, Sir.	Ek nazar dekhiye, sar.	एक नजर देखिये, सर
9. Shirts with novelty.	Nutantaa liye kameejen.	नूतनता लिए कमीजें...
10. Sixty rupees each.	Saath rupaye prati kameej	साठ रुपये प्रति कमीज
11. These are a little costlier.	Ye kuchh manhagee hain.	ये कुछ मंहगी हैं
12. Hundred rupees each.	Prati kameej sau rupaye.	प्रति कमीज सौ रुपये
13. Give me six pieces.	Mujhe ye chhah de deejiye.	मुझे ये छः दे दीजिए
14. For you madam, blouses?	Aapke liye, mohtarmaa, blaauj?	आपके लिए मोहतरमा ब्लाउज?
15. Let me have a look	Mujhe dekhne deejiye.	मुझे देखने दीजिए
16. Here are the varieties with novelty.	Ye raheen nutantaa ke sang vividhtaayen.	ये रहीं नूतनता के संग विविधतायें।
17. Give me these two.	Mujko ye do deejiye.	मुझको ये दो दीजिए
18. What more will you have?	Aur kyaa logi tum?	और क्या लोगी तुम ?
19. One maxy.	Ek maiksee.	एक मैक्सी
20. No saree?	Saree naheen?	साड़ी नहीं?
21. One, if your purse permits.	Ek, agar tumhaaraa pars kubool kare.	एक, अगर तुम्हारा पर्स कुबूल करे

XV LAUNDRY

1. My garments are dirty. — Mere kapre gande hain. — मेरे कपड़े गंदे हैं
2. I'm going to the laundry. — Main laundree jaa rahaa hoon. — मैं लाँड्री जा रहा हूँ
3. How much do you charge for dry-cleaning a suit? — Tum ek soot kee draau kleening kaa kyaa lete ho? — तुम एक सूट की ड्राय-चीलनिंग का क्या लेते हो ?
4. Twenty-five rupees, Sir. — Pachchees rupaye shreemanjee. — पच्चीस रुपये, श्रीमानू जी
5. And for washing pants and shirts? — Aur paintkameej kee dhulaaee kaa? — और पैंट-कमीज की धुलाई का ?
6. Rs. 1.50 per piece. — Prati pees derh rupaye. — प्रति पीस डेढ़ रुपये
7. And for ironing? — Aur istree karne kaa? — और इस्त्री करने का?
8. Fifty paise each. — Pachaas paise prati pees. — पचास पैसे प्रति पीस
9. Take this suit for dry-cleaning. — Yah soot draay-kleening ke liye lo. — यह सूट ड्राय-चीलनिंग के लिए लो
10. Thank you, Sir. — Dhanyavaad hai shree-maanjee. — धन्यवाद है, श्रीमान जी

11. After a week. — Ek saptaah bad — एक सप्ताह बाद
12. Take care, it should be properly dry-cleaned. — Khyaal rakhnaa, yah saaph dhulnaa chaahiye. — ख्याल रखना, यह साफ घुलना चाहिए
13. Please don't worry, Sir. I take the best care. — Ghabraaeeye mat, sar. Main pooree saavd-haanee barattaa hoon. — घबराईये मत, सर, मैं पूरी सावधानी बरतता हूँ।
14. Customer's satisfaction should be your motto. — Graahak kee santushti tumhaaraa dhyey honaa chaahiye. — ग्राहक की संतुष्टि तुम्हारा ध्येय होना चाहिए
15. Of course, mine is so, Sir — Sachmuch meraa dhyey yahee hai, sar. — सचमुच मेरा ध्येय यही है, सर।
16. Thank you. — Shukriyaa. — शुक्रिया, धन्यवाद।

PART 5

GRAMMAR
Chapter 1
Parts of Speech

1. Noun	Sangyaa	संज्ञा
2. Pronoun	Sarvanaam	सर्वनाम
3. Verb	Kriyaa	क्रिया
4. Adjective	Visheshan	विशेषण
5. Adverb	Kriyaa visheshan	क्रिया विशेषण
6. Conjunction	Samuchchay-bodhak avyay	समुच्चयबोधक अव्यय
7. Preposition	Sambandh-bodhak avyay	सम्बन्धबोधक अव्यय
8. Interjection	Vismayaadi-bodhak avyay	विस्मयादिबोधक अव्यय

I NOUNS kinds

1. Common noun	Jaativaachak sangyaa	जातिवाचक संज्ञा
2. Proper noun	Vyaktivaachak sangyaa	व्यक्तिवाचक संज्ञा
3. Collective noun	Samoohvaachak sangyaa	समूहवाचक संज्ञा
4. Material noun	Dravyavaachaksangyaa	द्रव्यवाचक संज्ञा
5. Abstract noun	Bhaavvaachak sangyaa	भाववाचक संज्ञा

Examples

1. Common noun

Cow	gaay;	गाय
Boy	larkaa;	लड़का

Crow	kauwaa;	कौआ
Fish	machhlee;	मछली
Ant	cheentee;	चींटी
Mango	aam;	आम
Potato	aaloo;	आलू
Book	kitaab;	किताब
Fan	pankhaa;	पंखा
House	ghar;	घर
Road	sarak;	सड़क
Park	paark;	पार्क
Radio	redio;	रेडियो
Sky	aakaash;	आकाश

Note: The name of anything in common is called a common noun.

2. Proper noun

Mohan	mohan	मोहन
Radha	radhaa	राधा
Nepal	nepaal	नेपाल
Bengal	bangaal	बंगाल
Ganges	gangaa	गंगा
Himalaya	himaalay	हिमालय
Atlantic	atlaantik	अटंलाटिक
America	amerikaa	अमेरिका
Bible	Baaibil	बाईबिल
Hindu	hindoo	हिन्दू

3. Collective noun

| Army | senaa; | सेना |
| Military | militree; | मिलिट्री |

Navy	jalsenaa;	जल सेना
Brigade	briged;	ब्रिगेड
Party	paartee;	पार्टी

Note: Anything in collection is called a collective noun.

4. Material noun

Oil	tel;	तेल
Petrol	petrol;	पैट्रोल
Butter	makkhan;	मक्खन
Milk	doodh;	दूध
Water	paanee	पानी

Note: Any liquid is called a material noun.

5. Abstract noun

Kindness	dayaalutaa;	दयालुता
Blindness	andhaapan;	अंधापन
Illness	beemaaree;	बीमारी
Ability	yogyataa;	योग्यता
Capability	kshamtaa;	क्षमता
Accuracy	yathaarthtaa;	यथार्थता
Alliance	sangathan	संगठन

II PRONOUNS

The Personal pronouns have five forms. These forms are identified by a *type* (or case) example :

Examples

1. I-type

| I | Main | मैं |
| He | Vahe | वह |

She	Vah	वह
We	Ham	हम
They	Vay	वे

2. Me-type

We	Ham	हम
Me	Main	मैं
Him	Usey	उसे
Her	Uska	उसका
Us	Hamien	हमें
Them	Unhey	उन्हें

3. Mine-type

Mine	Mera	मेरा
His	Uska	उसका
Hers	Uska	उसका
Ours	Hamara	हमारा
Theirs	Unka	उनका

4. My-type

M y	Mera	मेरा
His	Uska	उसका
Her	Uska	उसका
Our	Hamara	हमारा
Their	Unka	उनका

5. My Self-type

My Self	Apne ko	अपने को
Him Self	Aap hi	आप ही
Her Self	Aap hi	आप ही
Our Self	Apne Ko	अपने को
Our Selves	Apne Ko	अपने को

III VERBS

Am hun हूँ;- Is hain है, Are hai, hain है, हैं; Was thaa, thee था, थी; Were the, thee थे, थी।

N.B.: Above are auxiliary verbs (sahaayak kriyaayen).

Abandon (tr.)	tyaagnaa (sa.)	त्यागना (स.)
Abase (tr.)	maan ghataanaa (sa.)	मान घटाना (स.)
Abdicate (tr.)	pad/adhikaar tyaagnaa (sa.)	पद/अधिकार त्यागना (स.)
Abduct (tr.)	bhagaa le jaanaa (sa.)	भगा ले जाना (स.)
Abet (tr.)	bahkaanaa (sa.)	बहकाना (स.)
Abide (tr.)	maananaa (sa.)	मानना (स.)
Abjure (itr.)	shpath khaakar asveekaar karnaa (a.)	शपथ खाकर अस्वीकार करना (अ.)
Accede (itr.)	sweekaar karnaa (a.)	स्वीकार करना (अ.)
Accord (itr.)	milaan karnaa (a.)	मिलान करना (अ.)
Accrue (itr.)	laabhdaayak honaa (a.)	लाभदायक होना (अ.)
Accumulate (tr.)	dher lagaanaa (sa.)	ढेर लगाना (अ.)
Ache (itr.)	peeraa honaa (a.)	पीड़ा होना (स्.)
Achieve (tr.)	jeetnaa, praapt karnaa (sa.)	जीतना, प्राप्त करना (स.)
Acknowledge (tr.)	sweekaar karnaa (sa.)	स्वीकार करना (स.)
Act (itr.)	kaarya karnaa (a.)	कार्य करना (अ.)
Adapt (itr.)	yathaakaal vyasath karnaa (a.)	यथाकाल व्यवस्था करना (अ.)
Adjuge (tr.)	sthir karnaa (sa.)	स्थिर करना (अ.)
Administer (tr.)	shaasan karnaa (sa.)	शासन करना (स.)
Admit (tr.)	bhartee karnaa (sa.)	भरती करना (स.)
Adopt (tr.)	god lenaa (sa.)	गोद लेना (स.)

Advance (itr.)	age barhnaa (a.)	आगे बढ़ना (स.)
Adivise (tr.)	salaah denaa (sa.)	सलाह देना (स.)
Advocate (tr.)	vakaalat karnaa (sa.)	वकालत करना (स.)
Affect (tr.)	prabhaav daalnaa (sa.)	प्रभाव डालना (स.)
Affix (tr.)	jornaa, milaanaa (sa.)	जोड़ना, मिलाना (स.)
Aggress (itr.)	aakraman karnaa (a.)	आक्रमण करना (स.)
Allow (tr.)	anumati denaa (sa.)	अनुमति देना (स.)
Amaze (tr.)	chakit karnaa (sa.)	चकित करना (स.)
Amend (tr.)	shodhnaa (sa.)	शोधना (स.)
Animate (tr.)	jeevit karnaa (sa.)	जीवित करना (स.)
Annihilate (tr.)	lop karnaa (sa.)	लोप करना (स.)
Anticipate (tr.)	aashaa karnaa (sa.)	आशा करना (स.)
Apologize (tr.)	kshamaa maangnaa (sa.)	क्षमा मांगना (स.)
Apply (tr.)	niyukt karnaa (sa.)	नियुक्त करना (स.)
Appoint (tr.)	bahaal karnaa (sa.)	बहाल करना (स.)
Approve (tr.)	anumodan karnaa (sa.)	अनुमोदन करना (स.)
Argue (tr.)	bahas karnaa (sa.)	बहस करना (स.)
Arrange (tr.)	kram mein rakhnaa (sa.)	क्रम में रखना (स.)
Arrive (itr.)	pahunchnaa (a.)	पहुंचना (स.)
Aspire (tr.)	utkat ichchhaa karnaa (sa.)	उत्कट इच्छा करना (स.)
Assume (tr.)	anumaan karnaa (sa.)	अनुमान करना (स.)
Assure (tr.)	vishwaas karanaa (sa.)	विश्वास कराना (स.)
Attempt (tr.)	koshish karnaa (sa.)	कोशिश करना (स.)
Attract (tr.)	aakarshit karnaa (sa.)	आकर्षित करना (स.)
Avail (tr.)	kaam mein laanaa (sa.)	काम में लाना (स.)
Avert (tr.)	taalnaa (sa.)	टालना (स.)
Avoid (tr.)	parihaar karnaa (sa.)	परिहार करना (स.)
Awake (tr.)	jagaanaa (sa.)	जगाना (स.)

Awe (tr.)	bhay utpann karnaa (sa.)	भय उत्पन्न करना
Back (itr.)	peechhe jaanaa (a.)	पीछे जाना (स.)
Back (itr.)	peechhe hataanaa (sa.)	पीछे हटाना (स.)
Baffle (tr.)	unnati rokana (sa.)	उन्नति रोकना (स.)
Bait (tr.) (स.)	chaara dekar lalchaanaa (sa.)	चारा देकर ललचाना
Ban (tr.)	pratirodh karnaa (sa.)	प्रतिरोध करना (स.)
Base (tr.)	sthaapit karnaa (sa.)	स्थापित करना (स.)
Beat (tr.)	maarnaa, peetnaa (sa.)	मारना, पीटना (स.)
Befit (itr.)	yogya honaa (a.)	योग्य होना (स.)
Befog (tr.)	kuhre se dhaanpnaa (sa.)	कुहरे से ढांपना (स.)
Behold (tr.)	nihaarnaa (sa.)	निहारना (स.)
Beset (tr.)	gher lenaa (sa.)	घेर लेना (स.)
Beware (itr.)	saavdhaan honaa (a.)	सावधान होना (स.)
Bind (tr.)	baandhnaa (sa.)	बांधना (स.)
Bless (tr.)	aasheervaad denaa (sa.)	आशीर्वाद देना (स.)
Blow (itr.)	bahnaa (a.)	बहना (अ.)
Borrow (tr.)	udhaar lenaa (sa.)	उधार लेना
Boycott (tr.)	bahishkaar karnaa (sa.)	बहिष्कार करना (स.)
Brandish (tr.)	bhaanjnaa (sa.)	भांजना (स.)
Break (tr.)	tornaa (sa.)	तोड़ना (स.)
Bring (tr.)	laanaa (sa.)	लाना (स.)
Build (tr.)	nirmaan karnaa (sa.)	निर्माण करना (म.)
Burn (tr.)	tapaanaa (sa.)	तपाना (स.)
Buy (tr.)	khareednaa (sa.)	खरीदना (स.)
Cajole (tr.)	phuslaanaa (sa.)	फुसलाना (स.)
Calculate (tr.)	gananaa karnaa (sa.)	गणना करना (स.)
Call (tr.)	bulaanaa (sa.)	बुलाना (स.)
Care (itr.)	parvaah karnaa (a.)	परवाह करना (स.)

Caress (tr.)	laar karnaa (sa.)	लाड़ करना (स.)
Carry (tr.)	le jaanaa, dhonaa (sa.)	ले जाना, ढोना (स.)
Carve (tr.)	garhnaa (sa.)	गढ़ना (स.)
Cast (tr.)	dhaalnaa (sa.)	ढालना (स.)
Cater (itr.)	bhojan kaa prrabandh karnaa (a.)	भोजन का प्रबंध करना (स.)
Change (tr.)	parivartan karnaa (sa.)	परिवर्तन करना (स.)
Chant (tr, itr)	strot parhnaa (sa, a)	स्तोत्र पढ़ना (स.)
Chase (tr.)	peechhaa karnaa (sa.)	पीछा करना (स.)
Cheat (tr.)	dhokaa denaa (sa.)	धोखा देना (स.)
Chide (tr.)	daantnaa (sa.)	डाँटना (स.)
Cite (tr.)	pramaan denaa (sa.)	प्रमाण देना (स.)
Clasp (tr.)	lapetnaa (sa.)	लपेटना (स.)
Classify (tr.)	krambaddh karnaa (sa.)	क्रमबद्ध करना (स.)
Clean (tr.)	saaph karnaa (sa.)	साफ करना (स.)
Clothe (tr.)	kapraa pahanaanaa (sa.)	कपड़ा पहनाना (स.)
Collect (tr.)	jamaa karnaa (sa.)	जमा करना (स.)
Combine (tr.)	milaanaa (sa.)	मिलाना (स.)
Commence (tr.)	aarambh karnaa (sa.)	आरंभ करना (स.)
Commend (tr.)	prashansaa karnaa (sa.)	प्रशंसा करना (स.)
Commit (tr.)	samarpan karnaa (sa.)	समर्पण करना (स.)
Complete (tr.)	poorn karnaa (sa.)	पूर्ण करना (स.)
Compound (tr. itr.)	mishrit karnaa (sa.a.)	मिश्रित करना (स., अ.)
Compromise (tr.)	samjhautaa karnaa (sa.)	समझौता करना (स.)
Concentrate (tr. itr.)	ekaagra karnaa (sa, a.)	एकाग्र करना (स.)
Condole (itr.)	shok prakat karnaa (a.)	शोक प्रकट करना (स.)
Conduct (tr.)	aacharan karnaa (sa.)	आचरण करना (स.)
Construct (tr.)	nirmaan karnaa (sa.)	निर्माण करना (स.)

Convert (tr.)	badalnaa (sa.)	बदलना (स.)
Correct (tr.)	shuddh karnaa (sa.)	शुद्ध करना (स.)
Cover (tr.)	dhaanknaa (sa.)	ढांकना (स.)
Creep (itr.)	renganaa (a.)	रेंगना (स.)
Crush (tr., itr.)	kuchalnaa (tr. itr.)	कुचलना (स.)
Curse (tr. tir.)	shaap denaa (tr. itr.)	शाप देना (स., अ.)
Cut (tr.)	kaatnaa (sa.)	काटना (स.)
Dance (tr. itr.) (स., अ.)	naachnaa, nachaanaa (sa.a.)	नाचना, नचाना
Dare (itr.)	saahas karnaa (a.)	साहस करना (अ.)
Dazzle (tr.)	chakit karnaa (sa.)	चकित करना (स.)
Deal (tr.)	vyaapaar karnaa, vyavahaar karnaa (sa.)	व्यापार करना, व्यवहार करना(स.)
Declare (tr.)	ghoshanaa karnaa (sa.)	घोषणा करना(स.)
Defend (tr.)	rakshaa karnaa (sa.)	रक्षा करना (स.)
Deform (tr.)	kuroop banaana (sa.)	कुरूप बनाना (स.)
Delay (tr. itr.)	der karnaa (sa.,a.)	देर करना (स., अ.)
Demolish (tr.)	dhahaanaa (sa.)	ढाहना (स.)
Denude (tr.)	nangaa karnaa (sa.)	नंगा करना (स.)
Depute (tr.)	niyukta karnaa (sa.)	नियुक्त करना (स.)
Differ (itr.)	bhinna honaa (a.)	भिन्न होना (अ.)
Dilute (tr.)	patlaa karnaa (sa.)	पतला करना (स.)
Disappoint (tr.)	niraash karnaa (sa.)	निराश करना (स.)
Dismay (tr.)	hataash karnaa (sa.)	हताश करना (स.)
Displease (tr.)	naakhush karnaa (sa.)	नाखुश करना (स.)
Divide (tr., itr.)	khand karnaa, bhaag denaa (sa., a.)	खण्ड करना, भाग देना (स., अ.)
Divorce (tr.)	talaak denaa (sa.)	तलाक देना (स.)

Dominate (tr.)	prabhutwa darshaanaa (sa.)	प्रभुत्व दरशाना (स.)
Drag (tr.)	kheenchnaa (sa.)	खींचना (स.)
Drink (tr.)	peenaa (sa.)	पीना (स.)
Dwell (itr.)	nivaas karnaa (a.)	निवास करना (स.)
Edit (tr.)	sampaadan karnaa (sa.)	संपादन करना (स.)
Educate (tr.)	shikshit karnaa (sa.)	शिक्षित करना (स.)
Elect (tr.)	chunanaa (sa.)	चुनना (स.)
Employ (tr.)	niyukta karnaa (sa.)	नियुक्त करना (स.)
Enervate (tr.)	ksheen karnaa (sa.)	क्षीण करना (स.)
Enthral (tr.)	mohit karna (sa.)	मोहित करना (स.)
Entrap (tr.)	jaal men phasaanaa (sa.)	जाल में फंसाना (स.)
Erect (tr.) (स.)	banaanaa, unchaa karnaa (sa.)	बनाना, ऊँचा करना
Evade (tr., itr.)	hataanaa, vaakachhal karnaa (sa.aℓ)	हटाना, वाकूछल करना (स., अ.)
Excuse (tr.)	maaph karnaa (sa.)	माफ करना (स.)
Face (tr.)	saamnaa karnaa (sa.)	सामना करना (स.)
Fall (itr.)	girnaa (a.)	गिरना (अ.)
Favour (tr.)	kripaa karnaa (sa.)	कृपा करना (स.)
Follow (tr.)	anugaman karnaa (sa.)	अनुमगन करना (स.)
Forego (tr., itr.)	aage honaa, tyagnaa (sa., a.)	आगे होना, त्यागना (स., अ.)
Fry (tr.)	bhoonanaa, talanaa (sa.)	भूनना, तलना (स.)
Gamble (itr.)	jua khelnaa (a.)	जुआ खेलना (स.)
Gaze (itr.)	ghoorna (a.)	घूरना (अ.)

Glance (tr.)	nigah dalna (sa.)	निगाह डालना (स.)
Goad (tr.)	ankush lagaanaa (sa.)	अंकुश लगाना (स.)
Grind (tr.)	peesnaa (sa.)	पीसना (स.)
Hasten (itr.)	jaldee karnaa (a.)	जल्दी करना (अ.)
Help (tr.)	sahaayataa karnaa (sa.)	सहायता करना (स.)
Hiss (itr.)	phuphkaarnaa (a.)	फुफकारना (स.)
Huddle (tr.)	dher lagaanaa (sa.)	ढेर लगाना (स.)
Hurry (itr.)	jaldee karnaa (a.)	जल्दी करना (अ.)
Husk (tr.)	bhoosa hataanaa (sa.)	भूसा हटाना (स.)
Hypnotize (tr.)	rehan rakhnaa (sa.)	रेहन रखना (स.)
Idolize (tr.)	pooja karnaa (sa.)	पूजा करना (स.)
Illumine (tr.)	prajwalit karnaa (sa.)	प्रज्वलित करना (स.)
Impel (tr.)	pravrit karnaa (sa.)	प्रवृत्त करना (स.)
Inaugurate (tr.)	pratisthaan karnaa (sa.)	प्रतिष्ठान करना (स.)
Infer (tr.)	anumaan karnaa (sa.)	अनुमान करना (स.)
Invent (tr.)	aavishkaar karnaa (sa.)	अविष्कार करना (स.)
Joke (tr.)	majaak karnaa (a.)	मज़ाक करना (स.)
Kill (tr.)	hatyaa karnaa, jaan maarna (sa.)	हत्या करना, जान मारना (स.)
Land (itr.)	jahaaj se utarnaa (a.)	जहाज से उतरना (स.)
Laugh (itr.)	hansnaa (a.)	हंसना (स.)
Lose (tr.)	khonaa (sa.)	खोना (स.)
Lurk (itr.)	ghaat mein rahnaa (a.)	घात में रहना (स.)
Make (tr.)	banaanaa (sa.)	बनाना (स.)
Mark (tr.)	lakshya karnaa, mohar lagaanaa (sa.)	लक्ष्य करना, मोहर लगाना (स.)
Mean (itr.)	artha lagaanaa (a.)	अर्थ लगाना (स.)
Milk (tr.)	doodh duhanaa (sa.)	दूध दुहना (स.)

Modify (tr.)	sudhaarnaa (sa.)	सुधारना (स.)
Mutter (tr., itr.)	barbaraanaa (a.,sa.)	बड़बड़ाना (स.)
Nominate (tr.)	kisee pad ke liye nirdisht karnaa (sa.)	किसी पद के लिए निर्दिष्ट करना (स.)
Nullify (tr.)	viphal karnaa (sa.)	विफल करना (स.)
Oblige (tr.)	kritagya karnaa (sa.)	कृतज्ञ करना (स.)
Obtain (tr.)	praapt karnaa (sa.)	प्राप्त करना (स.)
Occupy (tr.)	adhikaar karnaa (sa.)	अधिकार करना (स.)
Offer (tr.)	pradaan karnaa (sa.)	प्रदान करना (स.)
Ornament (tr.)	alankrit karnaa (sa.)	अलंकृत करना (स.)
Outrage (tr.)	sateetva nasht karnaa (sa.)	सतीत्व नष्ट करना (स.)
Persecute (tr.)	peeraa denaa (sa.)	पीड़ा देना (स.)
Perturb (tr.)	vyagra karnaa (sa.)	व्यग्र करना (स.)
Precede (tr.,itr.)	aage jaanaa, poorva mein honaa (a.sa.)	आगे जाना, पूर्व में होना (अ.,स.)
Prevail (tr.)	prabal honaa (sa.)	प्रबल होना (स.)
Revive (tr. itr.)	phir se jeevit karnaa (a.,sa.)	फिर से जीवित करना (स., अ.)
Revolt (tr.)	balvaa karnaa (a.,sa.) (tr.,itr.)	बलवा करना (स., अ.)
Roast (tr.)	bhoonanaa, senkanaa (sa.)	भूनना, सेकना (स.)
Save (tr.)	bachaana (sa.)	बचाना (स.)
Sniff (tr. Itr.)	chheenknaa (sa.,a.)	छींकना (स., अ.
Stride (itr.)	udyam karnaa (a.)	उद्यम करना (अ.)

Note: tr. stands for transitive sakarmak सकर्मक (स.); itr stands for intransitive akarmak अकर्मक (अ.) ।

IV ADJECTIVES:

Able	yogya	योग्य
Accommodating	upkaaree, milansaar	उपकारी, मिलनसार
Acrid	teekhaa	तीखा
Adverse	vipreet	विपरीत
Afloat	bahtaa huvaa	बहता हुआ
Agog	gatimaan, aatur	गतिमान, आतुर
Alluvial	baarh se banaa huvaa	बाढ़ से बना हुआ
Amiable	mitravat	मित्रवत
Anonymous	gumnaam	गुमनाम
Apprehensive	vichaarvaan	विचारवान
Arrant	kukhyaat	कुख्यात
Astonishing	adbhut	अद्भुत
Attractive	aakarshak	आकर्षक
Augural	shakun sambandhee	शकुन संबंधी
Avaricious	laalchee	लालची
Awful	bhayaanak	भयानक
Baffling	ghabraanewaalaa	घबड़ाने वाला
Baneful	vishailaa	विषैला
Bankrupt	divaaliyaa	दिवालिया
Baseless	niraadhaar	निराधार
Bedrgabgled	burf ya keechar se gandaa kiyaa huvaa	बर्फ या कीचड़ से गंदा किया हुआ
Belligerent	laraakaa	लड़ाका
Bewitching	lubhaanewaalaa	लुभानेवाला
Blessed	bhaagyavaan	भाग्यवान
Bloody	nirdaee, hatyaaraa	निर्दयी, हताश

Bountiful	daansheel	दानशील
Brilliant	dedeepyamaan	दैदीप्यमान
Brutish	pashu ke samaan	पशु के समानं
Burlesque	haasyajanak	हास्यजनक
Cadaverous	shavtulya	शवतुल्य
Candid	nishkapat	निष्कपट
Capricious	asthir	अस्थिर
Celibate	brahmchaaree	ब्रह्मचारी
Civic	naagrik	नागरिक
Cheerless	mand, udaas	मन्द, उदास
Coherent	sambaddh	संबद्ध
Comical	thitholiyaa	ठिठोलिया
Conceivable	vichaarneeya	विचारणीय
Conjugal	daampatya	दामपत्य
Copulative	sanbhogkaaree	संभोगकारी
Cosmic	jagat-sambandhee	जगत संबंधी
Coward	darpok	डरपोक
Cryptic	gupta	गुप्त
Current	prachalit	प्रचलित
Cyclic	chakravaat	चक्रवात
Dazzling	chaundhiyaanewaalaa	चौंधियाने वाला
Debonair	vineet	विनीत
Defective	doshyukta	दोषयुक्त
Delusive	maayaavee	मायावी
Diffusive	phailaanewaalaa	फैलाने वाला.
Dogmatic	swamataabhimaanee	स्वमताभिमानी
Efficient	kaaryaksham	कार्यक्षम
Eloquent	vaakpatu	वाक्पटु

English	Transliteration	Hindi
Envious	eershyaalu	ईर्ष्यालु
Erosive	naash karnewaalaa	नाश करने वाला
Eternal	ananat	अनन्त
Eventual	antim	अन्तिम
Exhilarating	aanandadaayak	आनंददायक
Extraneous	asambaddh	असम्बद्ध
Facetious	kritrim	कृत्रिम
Felicitous	param sukhee	परम सुखी
Flabby	pilpilaa	पिलपिला
Formal	niyamaanusaar	नियमानुसार
Fraternal	bhraatri-sadrish	भ्रातृ-सदृश
Funny	khilwaaree	खिलवाड़ी
Gallant	bharkeelaa	भड़कीला
Gibbous	kubraa	कुबड़ा
Glistening	chamkeelaa	चमकीला
Gloomy	andhkaarmay	अंधकारमय
Gorgeous	chaundhaanewaalaa	चौंधाने वाला
Gruesome	bhayankar	भयंकर
Haggard	dublaa-patlaa	दुबला-पतला
Haughty	abhimaanee	अभिमानी
Hoarse	ruksha	रूक्ष
Hoggish	suar jaisaa	सुअर जैसा
Hospitable	aatithyakaaree	आतिथ्यकारी
Humorous	vinodee	विनोदी
Illicit	avaidh	अवैध
Illustrious	prakhyaat	प्रख्यात
Immodest	asabhya	असभ्य
Impermeable	apraveshya	अप्रवेश्य

Impolite	aneetigya	अनीतिज्ञ
Imprudent	avivekee	अविवेकी
Inauspicious	ashubh	अशुभ
Incohesive	asambaddh	असम्बद्ध
Incongruent	ayogya	अयोग्य
Indecorous	asabhya	असभ्य
Indisputable	nirvivaad	निर्विवाद
Inferior	nyoon, heen	न्यून, हीन
Irreligious	adharmee	अधर्मी
Inventive	aavishkaar	अविष्कार करने
	karne yogya	योग्य
Jubilant	praphullit	प्रफुल्लित
Juvenile	tarun	तरुण
Kinetic	gati sambandhee	गति संबंधी
Kingly	raajkeeya	राजकीय
Legitimate	auras	औरस
Lineal	paitrik	पैतृक
Literary	shaastreeya	शास्त्रीय
Livid	neele rang kaa	नीले रंग का
Lofty	oonchaa, unnat	ऊँचा, उन्नत
Loose	dheelaa	ढीला
Luminous	prakaashayukta	प्रकाशयुक्त
Luxurious	vilaasee	विलासी
Mammoth	mahaan	महान
Maniacal	jhakkee	झक्की
Melodious	madhur	मधुर
Mild	mridu	मृदु
Moderate	parimit	परिमित

Mythological	pauraanik	पौराणिक
Nefarious	neech, paapee	नीच, पापी
Noxious	ahitkaaree	अहितकारी
Nominal	naam maatra kaa	नाम मात्र का
Numerous	anek	अनेक
Opulent	sampanna	सम्पन्न
Original	maulik	मौलिक
Otiose	avyaavahaarik	अव्यावहारिक
Oval	andaakar	अण्डाकार
Painful	dukhadaayee	दुखदायी
Papal	pope sambandhee	पोप संबंधी
Passive	nishkriya	निष्क्रिय
Penal	dand vishavak	दण्ड विषयक
Penetrative	chhedak	छेदक
Peptic	paachak	पाचक
Persuasive	hridaygraahee	हदयग्राही
Pictorial	chitramay	चित्रमय
Remote	doorasth	दूरस्थ
Religious	dhaarmik	धार्मिक
Reputable	uttardaayee	उत्तरदायी
Scandalous	kalank lagaanewaalaa	कलंक लगाने वाला
Scant	sankuchit	संकुचित
Sickly	durbal	दुर्बल
Sincere	eemaandaar	ईमानदार
Sluggish	susta, dheemaa	सुस्त, धीमा
Solicitous	utsuk	उत्सुक

V ADVERBS

English	Transliteration	Hindi
Abeam	jahaaj kee shahteer par, aage kee or	जहाज की शहतीर पर, आगे की ओर
Abidingly	sthaayee roop se	स्थायी रूप से
Abjectly	neechtaa se	नीचता से
Abominably	ghinaunepan se	घिनौनेपन से
Abruptly	tatpartaa se	तत्परता सं
Accurately	shuddhtaa se	शुद्धता से
Actively	teevrataa se	तीव्रता
Allegorically	laakshnik roop se	लाक्षणिक रूप से
Amorously	kaamee-sadrish	कामी-सदृश
Anomalously	aniyamit roop se	अनियमित रूप से
Approximately	praayah shuddh roop se	प्रायः शुद्ध रूप से
Arbitrarily	swechchhaacharee roop se	स्वेच्छायारी रूप से
Astray	seedhe raaste se bhatakaa huaa	सीधे रास्ते से भटका हुआ
Audibly	spashta roop se	स्पष्ट रूप से
Bodingly	shakun se	शकुन से
Boorishly	asabhyataa se	असभ्यता से
Briefly	sankshep men	संक्षेप में
Brutishly	pashu kee tarah	पशु की तरह
Cheerly	prasannataa se	प्रसन्नता से
Circumspectively	saavadhaanee se	सावधानी से
Completely	poorna roop se	पूर्ण रूप से
Conveniently	suvidhaa se	सुविधा से
Creepingly	rengte hue	रेंगते हुए
Dangerously	bhayankar roop se	भयंकर रूप से
Decently	shishtataa se	शिष्टता से

Delayingly	vilamb karte hue	विलम्ब करते हुए
Dimly	dhundhlepan se	धुँधलेपन से
Divergently	vibhinnataa se	विभिन्नता से
Dwarfishly	naatepan se	नाटेपन से
Energetically	utsahpoorvak	उत्साहपूर्वक
Eventually	antatah	अन्ततः
Exactly	yathaavat	यथावत्
Expediently	yathochit roop se	यथोचित रूप से
Fairly	swachchhataa se	स्वच्छता से
Fastidiously	duraaraadhyataa se	दुराराध्यता से
Favourably	kripaa poorvak	कृपापूर्वक
Foul	apavitrataa se	अपवित्रता से
Gaspingly	haanphte hue	हाँफते हुए
Gruesomely	ghor roop se	घोर रूप से
Implicitly	nihasandeh	निःसंदेह
Indeed	vastutah	वस्तुतः
Inhumanly	kathortaa se	कठोरता से
Killingly	maarte hue	मारते हुए
Legally	kaanunee roop se	कानूनी रूप से
Luridly	bhayankartaa se	भयंकरता से
Miraculously	divya shakti se	दिव्य शक्ति से
Mournfully	shok-sahit	शोकसहित
Nominally	naam maatra se	नाम मात्र से
Notably	prasiddhi se	प्रसिद्धि से
Obligingly	anugrahpurvak	अनुग्रहपूर्वक
Onerously	bhaareepan se	भारीपन से
Outrageously	atyaachaarpurvak	अत्याचारपूर्वक
Pervasively	vyaapak roop se	व्यापक रूप से
Politely	vineet bhaav se	विनीत भाव से

Roaringly	garajte hue	गरजते हुए
Saucily	dhithaaee se	ढिठाई से
Simultaneously	ek hee saath	एक ही साथ
Socially	saamaajik roop se	सामाजिक रूप से
Steadily	sthirtaa se	स्थिरता से
Tangibly	spashta roop se	स्पष्ट रूप से
Thickly	aviral	अविरल
Traditionally	paramparaa ke dhang se	परम्परा के ढंग से
Willingly	prasannataa se	प्रसन्नता से
Wretchedly	deentaa se	दीनता से
Yieldingly	samarpan karte hue	समर्पण करते हुए

VI CONJUNCTIONS

Cumulative	yog-soochak	योग-सूचक
Alternative	chayan-soochak	चयन-सूचक
Adversative	virodh-soochak	विरोध-सूचक
Illative	parinaam-soochak	परिणाम-सूचक

Cumulative: And (aur) और, as well as (saath hee saath) साथ ही साथ, not only ... but also (sirph....naheen, balki, bhee) सिर्फ....नहीं, बल्कि....भी ।

Alternative: Either.....or (ya....ya....) या.......या....... neither....nor (na to) ना तो, else (anyathaa) अन्यथा, otherwise (naheen to) नहीं तो

Adversative: But (lekin) लेकिन, still (phir bhee) फिर भी, yet (tathaapi) तथापि, nevertheless (tispar bhee) तिसपर भी, however (jo bhee ho) जो भी हो, while (jab tak) जब तक, only (keval) केवल, whereas (jabki) जबकि

Illative: Therefore (atah) अतः, so (isliye) इसलिए, for (chunki) चूँकि, hence (etadarth) एतदर्थ, thus (is tarah) इस तरह

VII PREPOSITIONS

in	mein	में
with	se	से
of	kaa	का
within	bheetar	भीतर
for	ke liye	के लिए
before	pahle	पहले
to	ko	को
beside	alaavaa	अलावा
over	bhar men	भर में
among	beech men	बीच में
upon	oopar	ऊपर
since	lagaataar	लगातार
at	mein	में
after	baad	बाद
on	par	पर
into	andar	अंदर

VIII INTERJECTIONS

1. To exprress joy	harsh prakat karne ke liye:	हर्ष प्रकट करने के लिए
Ha! ha!... hurray!	vaah vaah shaabaash	वाह! वाह! शाबाश
2. To express grief	dukh prakat karne ke liye:	दुख प्रकट करने के लिए
Ah	aah	आह
O	O!	ओ!
Alas!	kaash!	काश!
3. To express approval	anumodan ke liye:	अनुमोदन के लिए
Bravo!	khub, bahut khub	खूब, बहुत खूब.

4. To express surprise:	aashcharya vyakt karne ke liye:	आश्चर्य व्यक्त करने के लिए
What!	kya!	क्या!
Indeed!	sachmuch!	सचमुच
Aha	aha	अहा
5. To attract attention:	dhyaan aakarshit karne ko:	ध्यान आर्षित करने को
Hark!	suno	सुनो!
Lo!	dekho	देखो
6. To address:	sambodhan karne ko:	संबोधन करने को
Ho!	ai jee	ऐ जी
Hello	hallo	हैलो

Chapter 3

Voice (Vachya)

| 1. Active Voice | kartre vaachya | कर्तृ वाच्य |
| 2. Passive Voice | karma vaachya | कर्म वाच्य |

Present Indefinite Tense

| Active: | I buy a book | main ek pustak khareedtaa hoon | मैं एक पुस्तक खरीदता हूँ |
| Passive: | A book is bought by me | mere dwaaraa ek pustak khareedee jaatee hai | मेरे द्वारा एक पुस्तक खरीदी जाती है |

Past Indefinite Tense

| Active: | The boy wrote a letter | larke ne ek patra likhaa thaa | लड़के ने एक पत्र लिखा था |
| Passive: | A letter was | laarke dwaaraa ek | लड़के द्वारा एक पत्र लिखा गया |

Future Indefinite Tense

Active:	That girl will read a novel	vah larkee ek upanyaas parhegee	वह लड़की एक उपन्यास पढ़ेगी
Passive:	A novel will be read by that girl	us larkee dwaaraa ek upanyas parhaa jaayega	उस लड़की द्वारा एक उपन्यास पढ़ा जायेगा

Present Continuous Tense

Active:	Ram is singing a song	Raam ek gaanaa gaa rahaa hai	राम एक गाना गा रहा है
Passive:	A song is being sung by Ram	Raam dwaaraa ek geet gaayaa jaa rahaa hai	राम द्वारा एक गीत गाया जा रहा है

Past Continuous Tense

Active:	Rekha was doing her work	Rekhaa apnaa kaam kar rahee thee	रेखा अपना काम कर रही थी
Passive:	Her work was being done by Rekha	Rkhaa dwaaraa apnaa kaam kiyaa jaa rahaa thaa	रेखा द्वारा अपना काम काम किया जा रहा था

Present Perfect Tense

Active:	I have done it	maine ise kar liyaa hai	मैंने इसे कर लिया है
Passive:	It has been done by me	yah mere dwaaraa kar liyaa gayaa hai	यह मेरे द्वारा कर लिया गया है

Past Perfect Tense

Active:	I had finished the work	maine kaam samaapt kar liyaa thaa	मैंने काम समाप्त कर लिया था
Passive:	The work had	kaam mere dwaaraa	काम मेरे द्वारा

| | been finished | samaapt kar | समाप्त कर |
| | by me | liyaa gayaa thaa | लिया गया था |

Future Perfect Tense

Active:	Sarla will have	Sarlaa bhojan	सरला भोजन कर
	taken the food	kar chukee hogee	चुकी होगी
Passive:	The food will	bhojan sarlaa	भोजन सरला
	have been taken	dwaaraa kiyaa jaa	द्वारा किया जा
	by Sarla	chukaa hogaa	चुका होगा

N.B.: No passive forms of Future Continuous & Perfect Continuous Tense.

Chapter 4

Number (Vachan)

| Singular | ekvachan | एकवचन | Plural | bahuvachan | बहुवचन |

Singular			**Plural**		
Singular	ekvachan	एकवचन	Plural	bahuvachan	बहुवचन
Boy	larkaa	लड़का	Boys	larke	लड़के
Girl	larkee	लड़की	Girls	larkiyaan	लड़कियां
Book	kitaab	किताब	Books	kitaaben	किताबें
Pen	kalam	कलम	Pens	kalmen	कलमें
Cow	gaay	गाय	Cows	gaayen	गायें
Class	shrenee	श्रेणी	Classes	shreniyaan	श्रेणियां
Kiss	chumban	चुम्बन	Kisses	chumban	चुम्बन
Watch	gharee	घड़ी	Watches	ghariyaan	घड़ियां
Brush	brush	ब्रुश	Brushes	brush	ब्रुश
Tax	shulk	शुल्क	Taxes	shulk	शुल्क
Mango	aam	आम	Mangoes	aam	आम

English	Hindi (roman)	Hindi	English	Hindi (roman)	Hindi
Potato	aalu	आलू	Potatoes	aalu	आलू
Cargo	kaargo	कारगो	Cargoes	kaargo	कारगो
Volcano	jwala-mukhee	ज्वालामुखी	Volcanoes	jwala-mukhee	ज्वालामुखी
Echo	pratishabd	प्रतिशब्द	Echos	pratishabd	प्रतिशब्द
Dynamo	daaynemo	डायनेमो	Dynamos	daaynemo	डायनेमा
Ratio	anupaat	अनुपात	Ratios	anupaat	अनुपात
Piano	piaano	पियानो	Pianos	piano	पियानो
Photo	photo	फोटो	Photos	photo	फोटो
Baby	bachchee	बच्ची	Babies	bachchiyaan	बच्चियां
Lady	mahilaa	महिला	Ladies	mahilaaen	महिलाएं
City	nagar	नगर	Cities	nagar	नगर
Story	kahaanee	कहानी	Stories	kahaaniyaan	कहानियां
Thief	chor	चोर	Thieves	chor	चोर
Wife	patnee	पत्नी	Wives	patniyan	पत्नियां
Life	jeevan	जीवन	Lives	jeevan	जीवन
Leaf	pattee	पत्ती	Leaves	pattiyaan	पत्तियां
Chief	pradhaan	प्रधान	Chiefs	pradhaan	प्रधान
Dwarf	baunaa	बौना	Dwarfs	baune	बौने
Proof	saboot	सबूत	Proofs	saboot	सबूत
Gulf	khaaee	खाई	Gulfs	khaaeeyaan	खाइयां
Grief	shok	शोक	Griefs	shok	शोक
Man	aadmee	आदमी	Men	aadmee	आदमी
Woman	stree	स्त्री	Women	streeyaan	स्त्रियां
Foot	paanv	पांव	Feet	paanv	पांव
Tooth	daant	दांत	Teeth	daant	दांत
Goose	battakh	बत्तख	Geese	battakhen	बत्तखें
Mouse	chooha	चूहा	Mouses	choohe	चुहे

| Ox | saand | सांड | Oxen | saand | सांड |
| Child | bachchaa | बच्चा | Children | bachche | बच्चे |

Singular & Plural alike

Swine	suar	सुअर
Deer	hiran	हिरन
Sheep	bher	भेड़
Dozen	darzan	दर्जन
Salmon	samudree machhlee	समुद्री मछली
Score	gananaa	गणना

Used Only in Plural

Scissors	kainchee	कैंची
Bellows	phephre	फेफड़े
Spectacles	chashme	चश्मे
Trousers	paajaame	पाजामे
Billiards	biliyard	बिलियार्ड
Thanks	dhanyavaad	धन्यवाद
Poultry	murgeepaalan	मुर्गीपालन
People	log	लोग

Used in Singular

Mathematics	ganit shaastra	गणित शास्त्र
Physics	bhautik shaastra	भौतिक शास्त्र
Politics	rajneeti	राजनीति
News	samachar	समाचार
Innings	inings	इनिंग्स
Mechanics	yantra vidya	यंत्रविद्या

Chapter 5
Gender (Ling)

Masculine puling पुलिंग   Feminine streeling स्त्रीलिंग

CHART

	Masculine			Feminine	
1. Bachelor	kunvaaraa	कुंआरा	Spinster	kunaaree	कुंआरी
2. Boy	larkaa	लड़का	Girl	larkee	लड़की
3. Brother	bhaaee	भाई	Sister	bahan	बहन
4. Bull	bail	बैल	Cow	gaay	गाय
5. Cock	murgaa	मुरगा	Hen	murgee	मुरगी
6. Dog	kuttaa	कुत्ता	Bitch	kutiyaa	कुतिया
7. Father	pitaa	पिता	Mother	maataa	माता
8. Gentleman	sajjan	सज्जन	Lady	mahilaa	महिला
9. Author	lekhak	लेखक	Authoress	lekhikaa	लेखिका
10. Giant	daitya	दैत्य	Giantess	daityaanee	दैत्यानी
11. Poet	kavi	कवि	Poetess	kavayitree	कवयित्री
12. Actor	abhinetaa	अभिनेता	Actress	abhinetree	अभिनेत्री
13. Emperor	samraat	सम्राट	Empress	samraa-gyee	सम्राज्ञी
14. Sorcerer	jaadugar	जादूगर	Sorceress	jaadu-garnee	जादूगरनी
15. Bullcalf	bachharaa	बछड़ा	Cowcalf	bachhya	बछिया
16. Cock	Murgaa	मुरगा	Hen	Murgi	मुर्गी
17. Hegoat	bakraa	बकरा	Shegoat	bakree	बकरी
18. Male sparrow	nar chidiya	नर चिड़िया	Female sparrow	maadaa chidiya	मादा चिड़िया

Chapter 6
Tense (kaal)

Present Tense	vartamaan kaal	वर्त्तमान काल
Past Tense	bhoot kaal	भूत काल
Future Tense	bhavishyat kaal	भविष्यत काल

1. Present Indefinite
   सामान्य वर्तमान
2. Present Continuous
3. Present Perfect
4. Present Perfect Continuous

1. Past Indefinite

2. Past Continuous
3. Past Perfect
4. Past Perfect Continuous

1. Future Indefinite

2. Future Continuous
3. Future Perfect
4. Future Perfect Continuous

CHART OF TENSES

	Indefinite	Continuous	Perfect	Perfect Continuous
Present	I read	I am reading	I have read	I have been reading
वर्तमान	मैं पढ़ता हूँ main parhtaa hoon	मैं पढ़ रहा हूँ main parh rahaa hoon	मैंने पढ़ा है maine parhaa hai	मैं पढ़ता रहा हूँ main parhtaa rahaa hoon
Past	I read	I was reading	I had read	I had been reading
भूत	मैंने पढ़ा maine parhaa thaa	मैं पढ़ रहा था main parh rahaa thaa	मैंने पढ़ा था main parhaa thaa	मैं पढ़ता रहा था main partha raha tha
Future	I shall read	I shall be reading	I shall have read	
भविष्यत्	मैं पढ़ूँगा main parhungaa	मैं पढ़ता रहूंगा main parhta rahoonga	मैं पढ़ चुका होऊंगा main parh chukaa hooongaa	

II. Pronouns

Personal	*Nominative*	*Objective*	*Possessive*
Ist Person	I मैं main	me मुझे, मुझको	my मेरा mera
प्रथम पुरुष		mujhe, mujhko	
	We हम ham	us हमें, हमको	our हमारा hamaaraa
		haman, hamko	
IInd Person	you तुम tum	you तुम्हें tumhen	your तुम्हारा tumhaaraa
मध्यम पुरुष	तुम लोग tumlog		
	आप aap आपलोग	तुमको tumko	आपका aapkaa
	aaplog आपको aapko		
IIIrd Person	He वह wah	him उसको usko	his उसका uskaa
अन्य पुरुष	She वह wah	her उसको usko	her उसका (uskaa)
	It यह yah	it इसको isko	its इसका iskaa
	They वे we	them उनको unko	thier उनका unkaa

Chapter 7

Clause (Upvakya)

Noun Clause	sangyaatmak upvaakya	संज्ञात्मक उपवाक्य
Adjective	visheshanaatmak	विशेषणात्मक
Clause	upvaakya	उपवाक्य
Adverb Clause	kriyaa-vishe shanaatmak	क्रिया-विशेषणात्मक
	upvaakya	उपवाक्य

EXAMPLES

Noun Clause

1. That he is honest	yah nishchit hai ki	यह निश्चित है कि
is certain	vah eemaandaar hai	वह ईमानदार है
2. This is what	jo kuchh usne	जो कुछ उसने कहा
he said	kahaa vah yah hai	वह यह है

3. The news that he has been arrested is wrong	yah khabar ki vah girphtaar kar liyaa gayaa hai, galat hai	यह खबर कि वह गिरफ्तार कर लिया गया है, गलत है

Adjective Clause

4. This is the pen that I bought yesterday	yah vahee kalam hai jo maine kal khareedaa thaa	यह वही कलम है जो मैंने कल खरीदा था
5. All accepted the proposal which I put yesterday	jo prastaav maine kal rakha thaa, sabne sweekaar kar liyaa thaa	जो प्रस्ताव मैंने कल रखा था, सबने स्वीकार कर लिया था

Adverb Clause

6. When I came he was not here	jab main aayaa, vah yahaan naheen thaa	जब मैं आया, वह यहां नहीं था
7. If she works hard, she will pass	agar vah parishram karegee to paas ho jaaygee	अगर वह परिश्रम करेगी, तो पास हो जायगी
8. He can run faster	vah adhik tej dour saktaa hai	वह अधिक तेज दौड़ सकता है
9. He is so weak that he cannot run	vah itnaa kamjor hai ki daur naheen saktaa	वह इतना कमजोर है कि दौड़ नहीं सकता
10 Walk carefully lest you should fall down	sambhal kar chalo, kaheen aisaa na ho ki gir paro	संभल कर चलो, कहीं ऐसा न हो कि गिर पड़ो

Chapter 8
Use of should, ought, must, lest, so that, may, might

English	Transliteration	Hindi
1. You should send a letter to him	apko uske paas patra bhejnaa chaahiye	आपको उसके पास पत्र भेजना चाहिये
2. He ought to serve his old parents	usko apne vriddh maataapitaa kee sevaa karnee chaahie	उसको अपने वृद्ध माता-पिता की सेवा करनी चाहिए
3. Vinod must come here	vinod ko yaahan awashya aanaa chaahye	विनोद को यहां अवश्य आना चाहिए
4. Walk slowly lest you should fall down	dheere-dheere chalo, aisaa na ho ki tum gir jaao	धीरे-धीरे चलो, ऐसा न हो कि तुम गिर जाओ
5. Work hard so that you may succeed	kathin parishram karo taaki paas ho jaao	कठोर परिश्रम करो ताकि पास हो जाओ
6. You may come in	tum andar aa sakte ho	तुम अंदर आ सकते हो
7. He ran fast so that he might catch the train	vah tej bhaagaa taaki relgaaree ko pakar sake	वह तेज भागा ताकि रेलगाड़ी को पकड़ सके

Chapter 9
Use of Causative Verbs

English	Transliteration	Hindi
1. The illiterate man has got a letter written	nirakshar manushya ne ek patra likhvaayaa hai	निरक्षर मनुष्य ने एक पत्र लिखवाया है
2. He had the dishes	usne mej par pyaali-	उसने मेज पर

laid on the table	yaan lagwaa deen.	प्यालियां लगवा दीं
3. I made the horse run fast	maine ghore ko tej dauraayaa	मैंने घोड़े को तेज दौड़ाया
4. He caused me to weep	usne mujhe rulaa diyaa	उसने मुझे रुला दिया

Chapter 10

Use of Gerund, Participle & Infinitive

Of gerund:	1. Singing is a good art	gaana aek sundar kalaa hai	गाना एक सुंदर कला है
	2. Drinking is not good for health	sharaab peenaa swaasthya ke liye achchhaa naheen hai	शराब पीना स्वास्थ्य के लिए अच्छा नहीं है
Of participle:	1. Barking dogs seldom bite	bhaunkne waale kutte kam hee kaatte hain	भौंकने वाले कुत्ते कम ही काटते हैं
	2. Hearing his voice I came out	uskee aawaaj sunkar main baahar aayaa	उसकी आवाज सुनकर मैं बाहर आया
Of infinitive:	1. To forgive is divine	kshamaa karnaa daivi hai	क्षमा करना दैवी है
	2. To err is human	bhool karnaa swaabhaavik hai	भूल करना स्वाभाविक है

Chapter 11
Use of Articles

1. Suresh is a boy	suresh ek larkaa hai	सुरेश एक लड़का है
2. Do not kill an ant even	cheentee tak ko na maaro	चींटी तक को न मारो
3. Boys are afraid of an elephant	bachche haathee se darte hain	बच्चे हाथी से डरते है
4. This is an interesting book	yah ek dilchasp kitaab hai	यह एक दिलचस्प किताब है
5. That is an owl	vah ek ulloo hai	वह एक उल्लू है
6. I have an umbrella	mere paas ek chhaataa hai	मेरे पास एक छाता है
7. The cow is a useful animal	gaay ek laabhkaaree pshu hai	गाय एक लाभकारी पशु है
8. It is an hour's work	yah ek ghante kaa kaam hai	यह एक घंटे का काम है
9. That is a horse	vah ek ghoraa hai	वह एक घोड़ा है
10. Always walk to the left	sadaiv baayen chalo	सदैव बाँए चलो
11. The Hindus regard the Ganges	Hindu log gaangaa ko maante hain	हिंदू लोग गंगा को मानते हैं
12. The camel is the ship of the desert	oont marusthal kaa jahaaj hai	ऊँट मरुस्थल का जहाज है
13. The poor are honest	gareeb eemaandaar hote hain	गरीब ईमानदार होते हैं
14. The Hindustan is a good newspaper	Hindustaan ek achchha samaachaar patra hai	हिन्दुस्तान एक अच्छा समाचार-पत्र है
15. English is the mother tongue of the English	Angrejee angrejon keea maatribhaashaa	अंग्रेजी अंग्रेजों की मातृभाषा है

Chapter 12

Use of Important Prepositions

1. He killed a bird with a gun — usne banduk se chiriyaan maaree — उसने बंदूक से चिड़िया मारी

2. The thief was caught by the police — chor pulis dwaaraaa pakraa gaya — चोर पुलिस द्वारा पकड़ा गया

3. Anil lives at Jammu — Anil jammoo men rahtaa hai — अनिल जम्मू में रहता है

4. Come in the office — daftar men aao — दफ्तर में आओ

5. The mad man jumped into the well — paagal aadmee kuen men kood paraa — पागल आदमी कुएं में कूद पड़ा

6. This is of no use — yah koee kaam kaa naheen hai — यह कोई काम का नहीं है

7. The rider fell of the horse — savaar ghore se gir gayaa — सवार घोड़े से गिर गया

8. Tell me about his fall — uske patan ke baare men mujhe bataao — उसके पतन के बारे में मुझे बताओ

9. There was a bridge over the canal — nahar ke oopar ek pul thaa — नहर के ऊपर एक पुल था

10. The dog was sleeping under the table — kuttaa mej ke neeche soyaa thaa — कुत्ता मेज के नीचे सोया था

11. Distribute the sweets between Ram and Shyam — mithaaee ko Raam aur Shyaam men baant do — मिठाई को राम और श्याम में बांट दो

12. My father distributed blankets among the beggars — mere pitaajee ne bhikhaariyon men kambal baante — मेरे पिताजी ने भिखारियों में कम्बल बांटे

13. He came here after the meeting was over	sabhaa samapt hone ke pashchaat wah yahaan aayaa	सभा समाप्त होने के पश्चात् वह यहां आया
14. He hid himself behind the school	vah skool ke peechhe chhip gayaa	वह स्कूल के पीछे छिप गया
15. He will die within a week	vah ek saptaah men mar jaaegaa	वह एक सप्ताह में मर जाएगा
16. He has been ill for four days	vah chaar dinon se beemaar hai	वह चार दिनों से बीमार है

Chapter 13

Use of Some Conjunctions

1. No sooner did he get up to deliver a speech than the hall resounded with clappings	jyonhee vah bhaasan dene ke liye uthaa, tyonhee bhavan taaliyon se goonj uthaa	ज्योंही वह भाषण देने के लिए उठा, त्योंही भवन तालियों से गूंज उठा
2. As soon as the bell rang, all the boys entered their classes	jyonhee ghantee bajee tyonhee sabhee larke kakshaaon mein chale gaye	ज्योंही घंटी बजी त्योंही सभी लड़के कक्षाओं में चले गए
3. We had hardly reached the school when the bell rang	ham mushkil se skool pahunche hee the ki ghantee baj uthee.	हम मुश्किल से स्कूल पहुंचे ही थे कि घंटी बज उठी
4. Scarcely had he gone out when it began to rain	vah mushkil se bahar niklaa hee thaa ki varshaa hone lagee	वह मुश्किल से बाहर निकला ही था कि वर्षा होने लगी

5. He is not only foolish, but also lazy	vah na keval moorkh hee hai, apitu susta bhee hai	वह न केवल मूर्ख ही है, अपितु सुस्त भी हैं
6. As you sow so shall you reap	jaisaa bovoge vaisaa kaatoge	जैसा बोओगे वैसा काटोगे
7. My book is as good as yours	meree pustak utnee hee achchhee hai jitnee ki tumhaaree	मेरी पुस्तक उतनी ही अच्छी है जितनी कि तुम्हारी
8. Rajan is not so handsome as his brother	Raajan itnaa sundar naheen hai jitnaa uskaa bhaee	राजन इतना सुंदर नहीं है जितना उसका भाई
9. Either do it or go away	yaa to ise karo yaa phir chale jaavo	या तो इसे करो या फिर चले जाओ
10. Neither you read nor do you let me read	na to tum parhte ho aur na mujhe parhne dete ho	न तो तुम पढ़ते हो और न मुझे पढ़ने देते हो

Chapter 14

Use of am to, is to, are to, was to, were to, has to, have to, had to, use to, used to, about to, instead of, begin to, how to, keep on, go on

1. I am to go	main jaanewaalaa hoon	मैं जानेवाला हूँ
2. She is to eat	vah khaanewaalee hai	वह खानेवाली है
3. Boys are to laugh	larke hansnewaale hain	लड़के हंसनेवाले हैं
4. Sohan was to collapse	sohan marnewaalaa thaa	सोहन मरनेवाला था
5. Boats were to capsize	naawen doobnewaalee theen	नावें डूबनेवाली थीं

6. He has to do work	usko kaam karnaa hai	उसको काम करना है
7. We have to finish it	hamen ise samaapt karnaa hai	हमें इसे समाप्त करना है
8. They had to quit	unhe chhorkar jaanaa paraa thaa	उन्हें छोड़कर जाना पड़ा था
9. We used to go on tours	ham paryatan par jaayaa karte hain	हम पर्यटन पर जाया करते हैं
10. He used to write to me	vah mujhe likhaa kartaa thaa	वह मुझे लिखा करता था
11. The train is about to leave	relgaaree khulnewaalee hai	रेलगाड़ी खुलनेवाली है
12. Youths read sex books instead of the Ramayana	naujaavaan raam-aayana ke badle yaun-pustaken parhte hain	नौजवान रामायण के बदले यौन-पुस्तकें पढ़ते हैं
13. I began to earn my bread	maine rotee kamaanee shuroo kee	मैंने रोटी कमानी शुरू की
14. He does not know how to swim	vah tairnaa naheen jaantaa hai	वह तैरना नहीं जानता है
15. People keep on crying	log rote rahate hain	लोग रोते रहते हैं
16. Leaders go on turning deaf ears.	leadear kaan bahare karte jaate hain	लीडर कान बहरे करते जाते हैं

Chapter 15

Sentences (Vakya)

Assertive	nishchaayatmak	निश्चयात्मक
Interrogative	prashnaatmak	प्रश्नात्मक

Imperative	aadeshaatmak	आदेशात्मक
Exclamatory	vismayaatmak	विस्मयात्मक
Optative	kaamnaatmak	कामनात्मक

1. Assertive Sentences

Ram says to me, "I am going home"	Ram mujhse kahtaa hai, "main ghar jaa rahaa hoon"	राम मुझसे कहता है ''मैं घर जा रहा हूँ''
Arun will say, "The boy swims in the river"	Arun kahegaa, "Larkaa nadee men tairtaa hai"	अरुण कहेगा ''लड़का नदी में तैरता है''
Rajesh told me that he wanted to go to Delhi	Rajesh ne mujhse kahaa ki vah Dillee jaanaa chaahtaa thaa.	राजेश ने मुझसे कहा कि वह दिल्ली जाना चाहता था

2. Interrogative Sentences

Am I mad?	kaya main paagal hun	क्या मैं पागल हूँ?
Is she a student?	kaya vah vidyaarthinee hai	क्या वह विद्यार्थिनी है?
Are they innocent?	kyaa ve nirdosh hain	क्या वे निर्दोष हैं?
Was Vijay working?	kaya vijay kam kar raha tha	क्या विजय काम कर रहा था?
Were they seeing a film?	kyaa ve philm dekh rahe the	क्या वे फिल्म देख रहे थे?
Shall Kamdeo leave India?	kyaa kamdev Bhaarat chhoregaa	क्या कामदेव भारत छोड़ेगा?
Will Radha come today?	kyaa Raadhaa aaj aaegee	क्या राधा आज आएगी?
Can he do this work?	kyaa vah yah kaam kar sakegaa	क्या वह यह काम कर सकेगा?

Could you not teach?	kyaa tum naheen parhaa sake?	क्या तुम नहीं पढ़ा सके?
Do you belong to Patna?	kyaa tum Patna ke rahnewaale ho	क्या तुम पटना के रहनेवाले हो?
Does Rohit not go tocinema	kyaa Rohit sinemaa naheen jaataa hai	क्या रोहित सिनेमा नहीं जाता है?
Did I not do it?	kyaa maine ise naheen kiyaa	क्या मैंने इसे नहीं किया
How are you my friend?	tum kaise ho mere mitra?	तुम कैसे हो मेरे मित्र?
What are you?	tum kyaa ho?	तुम क्या हो?
Who are you?	tum kaun ho?	तुम कौन हों?
What is your name?	tumhaaraa naam kyaa hai	तुम्हारा नाम क्या है?
When will she return?	vah kab lautegee	वह कब लौटेगी?
Where have the boys gone?	larke kahaan chale gae hain	लड़के कहां चले गए हैं?

3. Imperative Sentences

The teacher said, "Boys, sit down"	shikshak ne kahaa, "bachcho, baith jaao"	शिक्षक ने कहा, ''बच्चो, बैठ जाओ''
The Principal ordered the boys to stand up	principal ne larkon ko khare ho jaane kaa aadesh diyaa	प्रिंसिपल ने लड़कों को खड़े हो जाने का आदेश दिया
Mohan forbade his servant to go out	Mohan ne apne naukar ko baahar jaane se manaa kiyaa	मोहन ने अपने नौकर को बाहर जाने से मना किया
The beggar begged him alms	bhikhaaree ne usase bheekh maangee	भिखारी ने उससे भीख मांगी
His father advised him not to smoke	uske pitaa ne use dhoomrapaan naheen karne kee salaah dee	उसके पिता ने उसे धूम्रपान नहीं करने की सलाह दी

4. Exclamatory Sentences

Lila said, "Good-bye, my sister"	Leela ne kaha, "vidaee, meree bahan"	लीला ने कहा, ''विदाई, मेरी बहन''
The merchant said, "Alas! I am undone"	saudagar ne kahaa, "haae! main barbaad ho gayaa"	सौदागर ने कहा, ''हाय! मैं बर्बाद हो गया''
The captain said, "Bravo! well done"	kaptaan ne kahaa, "shaabaas! achchaa kiyaa"	कप्तान ने कहा, ''शाबाश! अच्छा किया''

5. Optative Sentences

The beggar said, "May God bless you!"	bhikhaaree ne kahaa, "bhagwaan tumhaaree khair kare"	भिखारी ने कहा, ''भगवान तुम्हारी खैर करे''
Rupa said, "May my happiness go to hell	Rupa ne kahaa, "meree khushee jahannum men jaae"	रूपा ने कहा, ''मेरी खुशी जहन्नुम में जाए''
He said, "Happy New Year to you"	usne kaha, "naya, saal tumhen mubaarak ho"	उसने कहा, ''नया साल तुम्हें मुबारक हो''

Chapter 16

Syntax (Vaakya Rachnaa)
1. SYNTAX OF NOUNS

(viii) The following are used as singular; 'a' and 'an' are not used before 'them'

Scenery	drishya	दृश्य
Information	soochnaa	सूचना
Business	kaarobaar	कारोबार

Poetry	kavitaa	कविता
Advice	salaah	सलाह
Furniture	farneechar	फर्नीचर
Luggage	saamaan	सामान
Offspring	santati	संतति
Mischief	apkaar	अपकार
Machinery	yantra	यंत्र

Exp.: The scenery is beautiful   drishya sundar hai   दृश्य सुंदर है

(ii) The following are used as singular:

News	samaachaar	समाचार
Politics	raajneeti	राजनीति
Physics	bhautik shaastra	भौतिक शास्त्र
Economics	arthashaastra	अर्थशास्त्र
Statistics	pariganan vidyaa	परिगणन विद्या
Mathematics	ganit shaastra	गणित शास्त्र

Exp.: This news is   yah khabar sach   यह खबर सच
not true   naheen hai   नहीं है

(iii) The followings are used as plural:

Thanks	dhanyavaad	धन्यवाद
Breeches	jaanghiyaa	जांघिया
Trousers	paayjaama	पायजामा
Spectacles	chashme	चश्मे
Assets	upakaran	उपकरण
Alms	bheekh	भीख

Exp.: Riches have   daulat ke pankh   दौलत के पंख
wings   hote hain   होते हैं

(iv) The following are used as both singular & plural:

| Sheep | bher | भेड़ |

Swine	suar	सुअर
Dozen	darzan	दर्जन
Cod	samudree machhlee	समुद्री मछली
Deer	hiran	हिरन
Pair	jora	जोड़ा

Exp.: The deer was lovely	hiran sundar thaa	हिरन सुंदर था
Many deer	bahut hiran	बहुत हिरन
were grazing	char rahe the	चर रहे थे

(v) The following are used as plural:

Cattle	maveshee	मवेशी
People	log	लोग
Gentry	kuleen jan	कुलीन जन
Poultry	murgeepaalan	मुर्गी पालन
Vermin	haanikaarak keere	हानिकारक कीड़े

Exp.: The people are sleeping	log so rahe hain	लोग सो रहे हैं

(vi) The followings are used as both singular & plural:

Tidings	vaartaa	वार्ता
Wages	wetan	वेतन
Means	saadhan	साधन

Exp.: The wages	paap kaa	पाप का पारिश्रमिक
of sin is	paarishramik	मौत है
death	maut hai	
The wages	paarishramik	पारिश्रमिक बढ़
have gone up	barh gaye hain	गये हैं

(vii) The following are used as singular:

| The Hindustan Times | दी हिंदुस्तान टाईम्स |
| The United States of America | दी युनाइटेड स्टेटस ऑफ अमेरिका |

Exp.:	The United States	Sanyukta Raajya	संयुक्त राज्य
	of America is	Amerikaa ek	अमेरिका एक
	a powerful	shaktishaalee	शक्तिशाली
	country	desh hai	देश है

(viii) The following are used as singular:
  Thirty rupees
  Hundred miles

| Exp.: | Hundred miles is | sau meel lambee | सौ मील लंबी |
| | a long distance | dooree hai | दूरी है |

(ix) Abstract & Material nouns are commonly used as singular:

Exp.:	Fish serves	machhlee bhojan	मछली भोजन के
	as food	ke roop men	रूप में काम
		kaam aatee hai	आती है

2. SYNTAX OF PRONOUNS

(i) Pronouns follow as per person, number, gender of their nouns:

Exp.:	Every man must	har aadmee ko	हर आदमी को
	keep his	apnaa vachan	अपना वचन
	promise	nibhaanaa chaahie	निभाना चाहिये
	All men must	sabhee aadmiyon	सभी आदमियों
	keep their	ko apne vachan	को अपने वचन
	promise	nibhaane chaahye	निभाने चाहिए

(ii) Pronouns must follow in order of persons as 2nd, 3rd & Ist:

| Exp.: | You, he and I | tum, vah aur main | तुम, वह और मैं |
| | are friends | dost hain | दोस्त हैं |

(iii) If the complement of 'to be' be a pronoun, then it's always the 'nominative case':

| Exp.: | It is I who am to blame | main hee doshee hoon | मैं ही दोषी हूँ |
| | If I he were I would not go | agar main vah hotaa to main naheen jaataa | अगर मैं वह होता तो मैं नहीं आता |

(iv) If a pronoun be an object of a verb or preposition, then it is always in the form of 'Objective case':

| Exp.: | These books are for me | ye kitaaben mere liye hain | ये किताबें मेरे लिए है |
| | Nobody will go there but him | uske sivaa koee vahaan naheen jaayegaa | उसके सिवा कोई वहां नहीं जायेगा |

(v) 'Who' and 'whom' are used for persons only:

| Exp.: | This is the girl whom I love. | yahee larkee hai jise main pyaar kartaa hoon | यही लड़की है जिसे मैं प्यार करता हूँ |
| | This is the boy who stood first | yahee larka hai jo pratham aayaa | यही लड़का है जो प्रथम आया |

(vi) 'which' stands for birds, animals and unlively things.

| Exp.: | The pen which I bought is lost | kalam jo maine khareedee thee, kho gaee | कलम जो मैंने खो गई खरीदी थी, |
| | The bird which I saw, flew away | chiriyaa jise maine dekhaa thaa, ur gayee | चिड़िया जिसे मैंने देखा था, उड़ गई |

(vii) Who kaun कौन is used as 'nominative case';

Whose kiska किसका kinka किनका is used as 'possessive case';

Whom jisko जिसको jinko जिनको is used as 'objective case'-

3. Syntax of Adjectives

(i) Adjective 'many a' is always used as singular:

Exp.:	Many a man	adhiktar aadmee	अधिकतर आदमी
	goes to see the Taj	Taj dekhne jaataa hai	ताज देखने जाता है

(ii) Little, a litle, the little have different uses and meanings:

Exp.:	He has little	uskee saphaltaa	उसकी सफलता
	chance of	kee ummeed	की उम्मीद कम
	success	kam hai	है
	A little knowledge	alpa gyaan khat-	अल्प ज्ञान
	is a dangerous thing	arnaak hotaa hai	खतरनाक होता है
	Ram wasted the	Ram ke paas jo	राम के पास जो
	little money	bhee thoraa pai-	भी थोड़ा पैसा
	he had.	saa thaaa, usne	था, उसने सब
		sab gawaan diyaa	गँवा दिया

(iii) Few, a few, the few have different meanings & uses:

Exp.:	He has few	uske koee dost	उसके कोई दोस्त
	friends	naheen hain	नहीं हैं
	He has read	usne kuchh upan-	उसने कुछ उपन्यास
	a few novels	yaas parhe hain	पढ़े हैं
	He gave away	uske paas jo bhee	उसके पास
	the few books	thoree kitaaben	जो भी थोड़ी
	he had	theen, usne	किताबें थीं, उसने
		sab de deen	सब दे दीं

4. Syntax of Verbs

(i) If nouns combined with 'and' convey about one person or thing, then singular verb follows:

Exp.: Rice and curry is	bhaat aur shorbaa	भात और
my favourite	meraa pyaaraa	शोरबा मेरा
food	bhojan hai	प्यारा भोजन है

(ii) If 'with', 'together with', 'as well as', 'besides' or 'like' combined with singular noun pronoun then singular verb follows:

Exp.: Ramesh with	Ramesh apne	रमेश अपने
(or together with	bhaaee ke saath	भाई के
or as well as) his	jaa rahaa thaa	साथ जा रहा था
brother was going.		
No one besides	Mahesh ke	महेश के अलावा
Mahesh is	alaawaa koee tee-	कोई तीक्ष्ण नहीं है
intelligent	kshna naheen hai	
Mohan like Sohan	Sohan jaisaa	सोहन जैसा मोहन
is industrious	mohan medh-	मेधावी है
	aavee hai	

(iii) If two singular subjects of 3rd persons be joined with either...or/ neither....nor, then singular verb follows:

Exp.: Neither Rita nor	na Reetaa, na	न रीता, न
Geeta was present	Geetaa upasthit thee	गीता उपस्थित थी

(iv) If the two subjects (one singular, the other plural) be joined with either...or/neither.....nor, then plural verb follows:

Exp.: Either the	shikshak yaa	शिक्षक, या उनके
teacher or his	unke chhaatra	छात्र क्लास में
students are	klaas men	उपस्थित हैं
in the class	upasthit hain	

Neither the	na to shikshak,	न तो शिक्षक, न
teacher, nor	na to unke chha-	तो उनके छात्र
his students	atra klaas men	क्लास में
are in the class	upasthist hain	उपस्थित हैं

(v) If two subjects of different persons are combined with either...or/neither...nor, then the verb will follow as per the latter person:

Exp.:	Either my father	yaa to mere pita-	या तो मेरे पिता
	or I am to do	ajee, yaa main is	जी, या मैं इस
	this work.	kaam ko karne-	काम को करने
		waalaa hoon	वाला हूँ
	Neither you	na to tum,	न तो तुम, न तो
	nor your	na to tumhaa-	तुम्हारी बहन ने
	sister has	ree bahan ne	इसे किया है
	done this	ise kiyaa hai	

(vi) Plural noun and plural verb follow after 'a great many'

	are in the class	upasthist hain	उपस्थित हैं
Exp.:	A great many	bahut se	बहुत से उम्मीदवार
	candidates have	ummeedvaar	चुने गये हैं
	been selected	chune gaye hain	

Chapter 17

Miscellaneous Exercises

Come into my room.	Mere kamre main aao	मेरे कमरे में आओ।
He was born	Tumse pahle	तुमसे पहले उसका
before you.	uskaa janm huaa thaa.	जन्म हुआ था।
He has one son.	Uske ek betaa hai.	उसके एक बेटा है।
Who lives there?	Wahaan kaun rahtaa hai?	वहाँ कौन रहता है?

When did he come?	Wah kab aaya?	वह कब आया?
When will you go again?	Tum phir kab jaaoge?	तुम फिर कब जाओगे?
You must not beat her	Tumhen usko maarnaa nahin chaahiye..	तुम्हें उसको मारना नहीं चाहिए।
I want to speak to you.	Main tumse kuchh baatcheet karnaa chaahtaa hoon.	मैं तुमसे कुछ बातचीत करना चाहता हूँ
I am displeased with you.	Main tumse aprasann hoon.	मैं तुमसे अप्रसन्न हूँ।
Do not disappoint me.	Mujhe niraash mat karo.	मुझे निराश मत करो।
I shall take rest.	Main aaraam loongaa.	मैं आराम लूँगा।
Is the air cool?	Hawaa thandhee hai?	हवा ठंडी है?
Come after dinner.	Bhojan ke baad aao.	भोजन के बाद आओ।
He wants you.	Wah tumko bulaataa hai.	वह तुमको बुलाता है।
London is bigger than Mumbai.	London Mumbai se baraa hai.	लंदन मुम्बई से बड़ा है।
Is this your house?	Yah tumhaaraa ghar hai?	यह तुम्हारा घर है?
What will you eat?	Aap kyaa khaaenge?	आप क्या खाएंगे?
Who has done this?	Yah kisne kiyaa hai?	यह किसने किया है?
What is your order?	Aapki aagya kyaa hai?	आपकी आज्ञा क्या है?
Are you at leisure?	Tumko awakaash hai?	तुमको अवकाश है?
Is this the very thing?	Kyaa yah vahee hai?	क्या यह वही है?
He is a fool.	Wah moorkh hai.	वह मूर्ख है।
Send them to my house.	Unko mere ghar bhej do.	उनको मेरे घर भेज दो।
He is a drunkard.	Wah sharaabi hai.	वह शराबी है।
What is your advice.	Tumhaari kyaa raay hai.	तुम्हारी क्या राय है।
What is the fare	Ek din kaa kya	एक दिन का क्या

for a day?	bhaaraa hai?	भाड़ा है?
This rupee is	Yah rupiyaa	यह रुपया खोटा है।
counter-feit.	khotaa hai.	
Who is the owner	Is ghar kaa maalik	इस घर का मालिक
of this house.	kaun hai?	कौन है।
He has no money.	Uske paas paisaa	उसके पास पैसा
	naheen hai	नहीं है?
I received your	Mujhe tumhaaree	मुझे तुम्हारी चिट्ठी
letter just now.	chittee abhee milee.	अभी मिली।
He is ready to go.	Wah jaane ko taiyaar hai.	वह जाने को तैयार है।
He has finished	Wah kaam kar	वह काम कर
his work.	chukaa hai.	चुका है।
Ask him his	Usse puchho ki uskaa	उससे पूछो कि उसका
name.	naam kyaa hai.	नाम क्या है।
He has come	Wah kaam ke liye	वह काम के
on business.	aayaa hai.	लिये आया है।
Throw away this cloth.	Yah kapraa phenk do.	यह कपड़ा फेंक दो।
Wait a little, he is	Zaraa thahro, woh	जरा ठहरो, वहं
putting on clothes.	kapre pahan raha hai.	कपड़े पहन रहा है।
He always drives	Wah apnee gaadee	वह अपनी गाड़ी
very fast.	sadaa tez chalaataa hai.	सदा तेज चलाता है।
Who is that person?	Wah wyakti kaun hai?	वह व्यक्ति कौन है?
Do you know the	Tum iska kaaran	तुम इसका कारण
cause of if?	jaante ho?	जानते हो?
I said nothing.	Main kuchh naheen bolaa.	मैं कुछ नहीं बोला।
What you say is all	Jo tum kahte ho sab	जो तुम कहते हो
true. Sir, it is not	sach hai. Mahaashaya,	सब सच है। महाशय,
my fault.	meraa dosh naheen hai.	मेरा दोष नहीं है।
I am fond of hunting.	Mujhe shikaar kaa shauk hai.	मुझे शिकार का शौक है।
I hope that	Mujhe aashaa hai ki	मुझे आशा है कि

English	Transliteration	Hindi
I have 400 rupees.	Mere paas chaar sau rupaye hain.	मेरे पास चार सौ रुपये हैं।
Give them two rupees each.	Unko do rupaye do.	उनको दो रुपये दो।
Look at that man.	Us manushya ko dekho.	उस मनुष्य को देखो।
Take a little walk in the garden.	Baagh men zaraa tahlo.	बाग में जरा टहलो।
This kind of fruit is plentiful here.	Is prakaar ke phal yahan bahut hain.	इस प्रकार के फल यहां बहुत हैं।
He wears spectacles.	Wah ainak lagaataa hai.	वह ऐनक लगाता है।
I cannot assist you.	Main tumhaaraa haath nahin bataa saktaa.	मैं तुम्हारा हाथ नहीं बटा सकता।
The allies will get success.	Mitron kee jeet hogi.	मित्रों की जीत होगी।
Thank God, I am quite well.	Iswar kee kripa se main bahut achchhaa hoon.	ईश्वर की कृपा से मैं बहुत अच्छा हूँ।
The time is over.	Samay ho chukaa.	समय हो चुका।
I am very glad to see you.	Apko dekhkar mujhe baraa harsh hotaa hai.	आपको देखकर मुझे बड़ा हर्ष होता है।
What did you say?	Aapne kyaa kahaa?	आपने क्या कहा?
I am afraid.	Mujhe dar hai.	मुझे डर है।
I thank you.	Main tumhen dhany-awaad detaa hoon.	मैं तुम्हें धन्यवाद देता हूँ।
I have heard nothing.	Maine kuchh naheen sunaa hai.	मैंने कुछ नहीं सुना है।
He has many friends.	Uske anek mitra hain.	उसके अनेक मित्र हैं।
He demanded ten rupees.	Usne das rupaye maange.	उसने दस रुपये मांगे।
Lock up the box.	Petee ko taalaa lagaao.	पेटी को ताला लगाओ।

Put a one rupee stamp on this letter.	Is chitthee par ek rupaye kaa tikat lagaao.	इस चिट्ठी पर एक रुपये का टिकट लगाओ।
Are your parents alive?	Tumhare maa-baap jeewit hain?	तुम्हारे मां-बाप जीवित हैं?
I shall punish him.	Main use dand doonga.	मैं उसे दंड दूँगा।
Why did you abuse him?	Tumne use kyon gaalee dee?	तुमने उसे क्यों गाली दी?
Why did you not ask leave?	Tumne chhuttee kyon na lee?	तुमने छुट्टी क्यों न ली?
He is a regular thief.	Wah pakkaa chor hai.	वह पक्का चोर है।
How far is the city from here?	Yahaan se shahar kitnee door hai?	यहाँ से शहर कितनी दूर है?
I waited for you.	Bahut der tak maine tumhaaree raah dekhee.	बहुत देर तक मैंने तुम्हारी राह देखी।
He has gone to Europe on leave.	Wah chuttee par wilaayat gayaa hai.	वह छुट्टी पर विलायत गया है।
How long has he been sick?	Wah kitne din se beemar hai?	वह कितने दिन से बीमार है।
What is the good of that?	Usse kyaa laabh hai?	उससे क्या लाभ है?
Where did you hear this news?	Tumne yah samaachar kahaan sunaa?	तुमने यह समाचार कहाँ सुना?
We are certain that you will be satisfied with the quality and price.	Hamen yakeen hai ki aap cheez aur dam se khush honge.	हमें यकीन है कि आप चीज और दाम से खुश होंगे।
We await your acknowledgment of the receipt.	Hum raseed kee pahunch kaa intizaar kar rahe hain.	हम रसीद की पहुँच का इन्तजार कर रहे हैं।
Unfortunately	Badkismatee se wah	बदकिस्मती से वह

English	Transliteration	Hindi
theyare in such a bad conditions that we cannot accept them.	itni kharaab haalat men hai ki ham manzoor naheen kar sakte.	इतनी ख़राब हालत में हैं कि हम मंजूर नहीं कर सकते।
Will you let us know what we can do for you in this matter?	Kyaa aap hamen bata yenge ki is maamle men ham aap ke liye kyaa kar sakte hain?	क्या आप हमें बताएंगे कि इस इस मामले में हम आपके लिए क्या कर सकते हैं?
We beg to inform you that the cotton sales have been in progress for a week.	Ham aap ko italaa dete hain ki ek hafte se ruee kee farokht ho rahee hai.	हम आप को इत्तला देते हैं कि एक हफ्ते से रुई की फरोख्त हो रही है।
We advice you to buy now (at once).	Ham aapko salaah dete hain ki aap fauran hi khareeden.	हम आप को सलाह देते हैं कि आप फौरन ही खरीदें।
The firm has been established for many years.	Yah karkhaanaa muddat se qaayam hai.	यह कारखाना मुद्दत से से कायम है।
Awaiting the favour of a reply.	Jawaab kee maiharbaa-nee kaa intizaar hai.	जवाब की मेहरबानी का इन्तजार है।
The money market is very firm.	Rupaye kaa baazaar bahut mazboot hai.	रुपए का बाजार बहुत मजबूत है।
We must be prepared for still dearer money.	Isse bhi mehenge rupaye ke liye hamen taiyaar rahanaa chaahiye.	इस से भी मंहगे रुपए के लिए हमें तैयार रहना चाहिए।
The value of the rice and wheat exported last week, amounted	Akhiree hafte baahaar bheje huye chaaval aur gehoon kee keemat	आखिरी हफ्ते बाहर भेजे हुए चावल और गेहूँ की कीमत पहले

to half a million	pahle hafte ke banisbat	हफ़्ते की बनिस्बत
rupees more than	paanch laakh rupaye	पाँच लाख रुपए
the previous week.	zyaadaa thee	ज्यादा थी ।
It is essential to	Yah nihaayat zaroori	यह निहायत जरूरी
ship the goods	hai ki maal kam se	है कि माल कम से
at the lowest	kam dar par jahaaz	कम दर पर जहाज
possible rate.	se bhejaa jaaye.	से भेजा जाए।
The date of the arrival	Aamad kee taareekh	आमद की तारीख
does not matter much.	kee koee baat naheen.	की कोई बात नहीं ।
Do not forget to	Maal kaa beemaa	माल का बीमा
insure the goods.	karnaa mat bhoolnaa.	करना मत भूलना ।
We think there will	Hamaaraa khyaal	हमारा ख्याल
shortly be a very	hai ki kuchh din men	है कि कुछ दिन में ही इस
great demand for	hee is mulk men ruee	मुल्क में रुई की
cotton in this country.	kee baree maang hogee.	बड़ी मांग होगी ।
Our persent supply	Hamaaraa maujudaa	हमारा मौजूदा
will not be sufficient	saamaan maang ke	सामान माँग के
to meet the demand.	liye kaafee na hogaa.	लिए काफी न होगा ।
We propose entering	Hamaaraa iraadaa	हमारा इरादा है कि
into another	hai ki aap ke saath	आपके साथ बराबर
speculation with	baraabar hisson	हिस्सों में एक और
you on equal terms	men ek aur sattaa karen.	सट्टा करें ।
We herewith send	Paanchvee taareekh	पांचवी तारीख को
you invoice for	ko mangvaaye	मंगवाये हुए माल
goods ordered	huye maal kee biltee	की बिल्टी हम
on the 5th.	ham bhejte hain.	भेजते हैं ।
We are sending	Ham aaj unhen jahaaz	हम आज उन्हें
them off by	se ravaanaa kar rahe	जहाज से रवाना
ship today.	hain.	कर रहे हैं ।
Where can I buy	Ve cheezen main	वे चीजें मैं कहाँ

those articles (things)?	kahaan khareed saktaa hoon?	खरीद सकता हूँ?
To whom do these parcels belong?	Ye paarsal kiskee hain?	ये पार्सल किसकी हैं?
Is he any relation of yours.	Kyaa wah tumhaaraa rishtedaar hai?	क्या वह तुम्हारा रिश्तेदार है?
What are you doing here?	Tum yahaan kyaa kar rahe ho?	तुम यहाँ क्या कर रहे हो?
I know what I have to do.	Main jaantaa hoon ki mujhee kyaa karnaa hai.	मैं जानता हूँ कि मुझे क्या करना है?
I understand you quite well.	Main tumhen theek thaak samajhtaa hoon.	मैं तुम्हें ठीक-ठाक समझता हूँ।
Now I know what to say.	Ab main jaantaa hoon ki kyaa kahun.	अब मैं जानता हूँ कि क्या कहूँ।
Someone must do it.	kisee na kisee ko yah karnaa chaahiye.	किसी न किसी को यह करना चाहिए।
I believe there is no one at home.	Meraa yakeen hai ki ghar par koi naheen hai.	मेरा यकीन है कि घर पर कोई नहीं है।
He must have about three hundred rupees in hand.	Uske paas kareeb teen sau rupaye. honge	उसके पास करीब तीन सौ रुपए होंगे।
There were about two hundred people present.	Koi do sau aadmi maoojud the.	कोई दो सौ आदमी मौजूद थे।
Some house or other must be vacant.	Koi na koi makan zaroor khaali hogaa.	कोई न कोई मकान जरूर खाली होगा।
This house compared with that house, is more beautiful.	Us ghar ke mukabule yah ghar zyaadaa khoobsoorat hai.	उस घर के मुकाबले यह घर ज्यादा खूबसूरत है।
These two books	Ye do kitaaben	ये दो किताबें

English	Transliteration	Hindi
are quite different.	bilkul alag hain.	बिलकुल अलग हैं।
The one is much	Ek doosri se bahut	एक दूसरी से
larger than the other.	baree hai.	बहुत बड़ी है।
Go, otherwise	Jaao, naheen to	जाओ, नहीं तो
you will catch cold.	tumko sardee hogee.	तुमको सर्दी होगी।
We know it all.	Ham yah sab jaante hain.	हम यह सब जानते हैं।
Hang up this lamp.	Yah battee latkaa do.	यह बत्ती लटका दो।
It is very late,	Bahut der hui, chalo	बहुत देर हुई,
let us go home.	ham ghar chalen.	चलो हम घर चलें।
You go on, we	Tum aage jaao, ham	तुम आगे जाओ,
are coming.	peechhe aa rahe hain.	हम पीछे आ रहे हैं।
Does the climate	Yahaan kee ab-o-	यहाँ की आबोहवा
of this place agree	hawaa tumko anukool	तुमको अनुकूल है?
with you?	hai?	
This depends	Yah aap par	यह आप पर निर्भर
upon you.	nirbhar hai.	है।
Have you ever	Aap kabhi	आप कभी दिल्ली
been to Delhi?	Dillee gaye hain?	गए हैं?
I do not know	Main usko naheen	मैं उसको नहीं
him.	pahchaantaa.	पहचानता।
Can you write?	Tum likh sakte ho?	तुम लिख सकते हो?
He beat his wife.	Usne apnee patnee	उसने अपनी पत्नी
	ko maaraa	को मारा।
How long have	Aap kitne din se	आप कितने दिन
you been in India?	Hindustaan men hain?	से हिन्दुस्तान में हैं?
What is your	Tumhaaraa aashay	तुम्हारा आशय
intention?	kyaa hai?	क्या है?
Send for him quickly.	Use jaldee bulaa-bhejo.	उसे जल्दी बुला-भेजो।
How you came	Tumne use kaise	तुमने उसे कैसे

to know that?	jaan liyaa?	जान लिया?
Change the water daily.	pratidin paani badlo	प्रतिदिन पानी बदलो।
Take this rubbish away.	Yah kooraa karkat le jaao.	यह कूड़ा-करकट ले जाओ।
What does it resemble?	Yah kis se miltaa hai?	यह किस से मिलता है?
I shall fine you.	Main tumhen dand doonga.	मैं तुम्हें दण्ड दुंगा।
Let him go out.	Usko bahaar jaane do	उसको बाहर जाने दो।
Let him come in	Usko andar aane do.	उसको अन्दर जाने दो।
Do it today instead of tomorrow.	Kal ke badle aaj karo.	कल के बदले आज करो।
Where does Mr. Bell live?	Bell mahaashay kahaan rahte hain?	बेल महाशय कहाँ रहते हैं?
This book is very good.	Yah pustak bahut achchhee hai.	यह पुस्तक बहुत अच्छी है।
What is the name of your wife?	Tumhaaree patnee kaa naam kyaa hai?	तुम्हारी पत्नी का नाम क्या है?
Where were you yestrday?	Kal tum kahaan the?	कल तुम कहाँ थे?
What is this thing?	Yah cheez kyaa hai?	यह चीज क्या है?
Who are these people?	Yah kaun log hain?	यह कौन लोग हैं?
My friend lives with me.	Meraa mitra mere saath rahtaa hai.	मेरा मित्र मेरे साथ रहता है।
What did you eat today?	Aaj tum ne kyaa khaayaa?	आज तुमने क्या खाया?
What can you do?	Tum kyaa kar sakte ho?	तुम क्या कर सकते हो?
I do not remember.	Mujhe yaad naheen hai.	मुझे याद नहीं है।
Is it necessary.	Yah zurooree hai	यह जरूरी है।
I am tired.	Main thakaa hoon	मैं थका हूँ।
	Main thakee hoon.	मैं थकी हूँ।
I cannot hear.	Main naheen sun sakataa.	मैं नहीं सुन सकता।

English	Transliteration	Hindi
I cannot see.	Main naheen dekh sakataa.	मैं नहीं देख सकता।
What is it called?	Isko kyaa kahate hain?	इसको क्या कहते हैं?
How beautiful.	Kaisa sundar.	कैसा सुन्दर।
Will you tell me?	Kyaa aap mujhe bataavenge?	क्या आप मुझे बतावेंगे?
It is all the same to me.	Mere liye yah sab baraabar hai.	मेरे लिये यह सब बराबर है।
What is the matter?	Kyaa baat hai?	क्या बात है?
What is it about?	Yah kis baare men hai?	यह किस बारे में है?
It is a mistake.	Yah galatee hai.	यह गलती है।
Whose mistake?	Kiskee galatee?	किसकी गलती?
What is to be done?	Kyaa kiyaa jaave?	क्या किया जावे?
I do not know.	Main naheen jaanataa.	मैं नहीं जानता।
Do you understand?	Kya aap samajhate hain?	क्या आप समझते हैं?
Do you not understand?	Kyaa aap naheen samajhate?	क्या आप नहीं समझते?
What do you want?	Aapko kyaa chaahiye?	आपको क्या चाहिये?
I do not want.	Mujhe naheen chaahiye.	मुझे नहीं चाहिये।
Leave me alone.	Mujhe akele chhod deejiye.	मुझे अकेले छोड़ दीजिये।
Have we got time?	Kyaa hamaare paas samay hai?	क्या हमारे पास समय है?
How much time will it take?	Ismen kitanaa samay lagegaa?	इसमें कितना समय लगेगा?
When do we start?	Ham kab ravaanaa honge?	हम कब रवाना होंगे?
When do we reach?	Ham kab pahunchenge?	हम कब पहुँचेंगे?
Where do we meet?	Ham log kahaan milenge?	हम लोग कहाँ मिलेंगे?

When shall we be back?	Ham kab vaapis aavenge?	हम कब वापस आवेंगे?
Who will take us there?	Hamako vahaan kaunaa le jaavegaa?	हमको वहाँ कौन ले जावेगा?
Do not go away.	Chale na jaaiye.	चले न जाइये।
Where have you come from?	Aap kahaan se aaye hain?	आप कहाँ से आये हैं?
What for?	Kisliye?	किसलिये?
Where to?	Kahaan ko?	कहाँ को?
Who has sent you?	Aap ko kisane bhejaa hai?	आपको किसने भेजा है?
I am in a hurry.	Main jaldee main hoon.	मैं जल्दी में हूँ।
I am late.	Mujhe der ho ga-ee.	मुझे देर हो गई।
Are you going anywhere?	Kya aap kaheen bahar jaa-rahe hain?	क्या आप कहीं बाहर जा रहे हैं।
Without a doubt.	Bina shak.	बिना शक।
You are joking.	Aap mazaak kar rahe hain.	आप मजाक कर रहे हैं।
I am not joking.	Main mazaak naheen kar raha hoon	मैं मजाक नहीं कर रहा हूँ।
I shall try.	Main koshish karoongaa.	मैं कोशिश करूँगा
I do not promise.	Main vaadaa naheen karata.	मैं वादा नहीं करता।
How do you feel?	Aap kee tabeeyat kaisee hai?	आपकी तबीयत कैसी है।
I am so sorry.	Mujhe bahut afasos hai.	मुझे बहुत अफसोस है।
It was not your fault.	Yah aapaka kasoor naheen thaa.	यह आपका कसूर नहीं था।
It was by mistake.	Yah galatee se ho gaya	यह गलती से हो गया।
What do you want?	Aap kya chaahate hain?	आप क्या चाहते हैं?
I want a room.	Main ek kamara chahata hoon.	मैं एक कमरा चाहता हूँ।

I want breakfast.	Main breakfast chahataa hoon.	मैं ब्रेकफास्ट चाहता हूँ।
I want to rest.	Main aaraam karana chaahata hoon	मैं आराम करना चाहता हूँ।
I want to go to the market.	Main bazar jaana chaahata hoon.	मैं बाज़ार जाना चाहता हूँ।
I want to see a good film.	Main achchhee film dekhanaa chaahataa hoon.	मैं अच्छी फिल्म देखना चाहता हूँ।
Please wait.	Kripaya intazaar kejiye.	कृपया इंतजार कीजिये।
Please take me to the aerodrome.	Kripaya mujhe hawa-ee adde par le chaliye.	कृपया मुझे हवाई अड्डे पर ले चलिये।
Please take me to the railway station.	Kripaya mujhe railway station le chaliye.	कृपया मुझे रेलवे स्टेशन ले चलिये।
I am obliged to you.	Main: aapaka aabhaaree hoon.	मैं आपका आभारी हूँ।
It is very kind of you.	Yah aapakee bahut kripa hai.	यह आपकी बहुत कृपा है।
I pray to God, you may have a comfortable journey.	Main Ishwar se praarthana karata hoo ki aap ki yatra sukh dayak ho.	मैं ईश्वर से प्रार्थना करता हूँ। कि आपकी यात्रा सुखदायक हो।
Come in please.	Kripaya andar aa-i-ye.	कृपया अन्दर आइये।
Please sit down.	Kripaya baith jaa-i-ye.	कृपया बैठ जाइये।
Please have a cold drink.	Kripaya kuchh thanda leejiye.	कृपया कुछ ठंडा लीजिये।
May I phone?	Kya main phone kar loon?	क्या मैं फोन कर लूँ?
May I sit here?	Kya main yahaan baith jaaoon?	क्या मैं यहाँ बैठ जाऊँ?

You may come in.	Aaap andar aa sakate hain.	आप अन्दर आ सकते हैं ।
You may go.	Aap ja sakate hain.	आप आ सकते हैं ।
newspaper please?	aapaka akhabaar le sakata hoon?	अखबार ले सकता हूँ ।
How old are you?	Aapakee kya umra hai?	आपकी कया उम्र है?
I am twenty-six years old.	Main chhabbees saal ka hoon.	मैं छब्बीस साल का हूँ ।
I want one more pillow.	Mujhe ek takiyaa aur chaahiye.	मुझे एक तकिया और चाहिए ।
We leave early tomorrow.	Ham kal subah jaldee chale jaan-vege.	हम कल सुबह जल्दी चले जावेंगे ।
I want these things washed.	Main in cheezon ko dhulavaana chaahata hoon.	मैं इन चीजों को धुलवाना चाहता हूँ ।
Do you take your tea with sugar or without sugar.	Aap chaay men cheenee lete hain ya bina cheenee ke.	आप चाय में चीनी लेते हैं या बिना चीनी की ।
Where is a good restaurant here?	Yahaan achchha restaruant kahaan hai?	यहाँ अच्छा रेस्टोरेन्ट कहाँ है?
Is lunch ready?	Kya lunch taiyaar hai?	क्या लंच तैयार है?
What time is dinner?	Raat ka khaana kitne baje hotaa hai?	रात का खाना कितने बजे होता है?
What is the price?	Kya keemat hai?	क्या कीमत है?
We shall dine at 9 p.m.	Ham raat ko nau baje khaana khaavenge.	हम रात को नौ बजे खाना खावेंगे ।
He is my friend.	Vah mere mitr hain.	वह मेरे मित्र हैं ।
Where does he live?	Vah kahaan rahate hain?	वह कहाँ रहते हैं?
What is the price?	Kya keemat hai?	क्या कीमत है?

English	Transliteration	Hindi
Show me another variety.	Mujhe aur maal dekheiye.	मुझे और माल दिखाइये।
How long does the train at the railway station?	Station par gaadee kitanee der thaharatee hai?	स्टेशन पर गाड़ी कितनी देर ठहरती है।
Is it an express train?	Kya yah express gaadee hai?	क्या यह एक एक्सप्रेस गाड़ी है?
Is it a passenger train?	Kya yah gaadee passenger hai?	क्या यह पैसेन्जर गाड़ी है?
Is the train on time?	Kya gaadee theek samay par hai?	क्या गाड़ी ठीक समय पर है?
Take me to the aerodrome.	Mujhe havaa-ee adde par le chaliye.	मुझे हवाई अड्डे पर ले चलिये।
Where can I get a place ticket?	Mujhe havaa-ee jahaaz ka ticket kahaan milega?	मुझे हवाई जहाज का टिकट कहाँ मिलेगा।
Which day you want to return?	Aap kis din lautana chaahate hain?	आप किस दिन लौटना चाहते हैं?
We need two seats.	Hamen do seat chaahiye.	हमें दो सीट चाहिये।
I am very sorry.	Mujhe bahut afasos hai.	मुझे बहुत अफसोस है।
It does not matter.	Ko-ee baat naheen.	कोई बात नहीं!
There is no harm done.	Ko-ee haani naheen hai.	कोई हानि नहीं है।
You are very kind.	Aapakee bahut kripa hai.	आपकी बहुत कृपा है।
Excuse me please.	Kripaya mujhe kshama karen.	कृपया मुझे क्षमा करें।
Good morning Mr. A.	Namaskaar or Namaste Mr. A	नमस्कार or नमस्ते Mr. A.
How do you do?	Aap kaise hain?	आप कैसे हैं?
How are you?	Aap kaise hain?	आप कैसे हैं?
How are you getting on?	Aap ka kaam kaisa chal rahaa hai?	आपका काम कैसा चल रहा है?

English	Transliteration	Hindi
Quite well, thank you.	Bilkul theek, dhanyavaad.	बिल्कुल ठीक, धन्यवाद।
It is a long time since we met.	Bahut dinon baad mile hain.	बहुत दिनों के बाद मिले हैं।
How do you feel?	Aap kee tabeeyat kaisee hai?	आपकी तबीयत कैसी है
I am not quite well.	Main bilkul theek naheen hoon.	मैं बिल्कुल ठीक नहीं हूँ।
Where is a good restaurant here?	Yahaan achchha restaurant kahaan hai?	यहाँ अच्छा रेस्टोरेन्ट कहा है?
Come in please.	Kripaya andar a-i-ye.	कृपया अन्दर आइये।
Please sit down.	Kripaya baith jaa-i-ye.	कृपया बैठ जाइये।
This way please.	Kripaya is taraf.	कृपया इस तरफ।
Please have tea.	Kripaya chaay peejiye.	कृपया चाय पीजिये।
A cup of tea.	Ek pyaala chaaya ka.	एक प्याला चाय का।
A cup of coffee.	Ek pyaala coffee ka.	एक प्याला कौफी का।
Have you had breakfast	Aapane naashta kar liya?.	आपने नाश्ता कर लिया?
Not yet.	Abhee naheen.	अभी नहीं।
Let us have breakfast together.	Ham log ek saath naashta karen.	हम लोग एक साथ नाश्ता करें।
The breakfast is ready.	Naashta taiyaaar hai.	नाश्ता तैयार है।
greetings to you.	shubh kamanaen.	शुभ कामनाएं।
Id Mubarik.	Ed mubarak	ईद मुबारक।
Many happy returns of the day.	Ishwar kare yeh shub din bar-bar aay.	ईश्वर करे यह शुभ दिन बार-बार आवे।